SpringerBriefs in Education

Citizenship Education for the 21st Century

Series Editor

Kerry J. Kennedy, Department of Curriculum and Instruction, The Education University of Hong Kong, Hong Kong, China

In all countries citizenship education (with a variety of different subject names) is a component of the school curriculum. Sometimes it is a school subject, sometimes a cross curriculum theme and sometimes it is focused on extra-curricular activities. Its purpose, in whatever form it takes, is to prepare students to become future citizens. This is as true in democratic societies as it is in authoritarian societies. Visions for the role of citizens in different societies will differ but irrespective of the vision, the role of citizenship education is to support it and prepare young people for the role they are expected to play in the future. Currently, however, there are two key issues that make the expected role of citizenship education problematic. First, the function of citizenship education appears simple: support the values of the society of which young people are a part, equip them with the necessary skills for involvement in that society and ensure that on graduation students can play the role expected of them. Yet even though schools may do all they can to perform this role, they are not the only influence on students. It is acknowledged that such influences are multiple: parents, peers, and traditional media being amongst the most important. More recently social media have been shown to influence students in different ways. Thus school purposes for citizenship education may have to contend with competing values, making it difficult to achieve agreed outcomes for all students. Second, the broad macro context that characterises most societies have become more unstable and unpredictable. Contentious politics, international terrorism, populism, rising nationalism, fundamentalisms of different kinds and globalizaton all serve to fragment societies and detract from social cohesion. The common vision that is meant to bind societies, and hence form the basis of citizenship education, is thus under threat from different directions. Global values, versus national values, religious values versus secular values, multicultural values versus monocultural values, liberal values versus conservative values: it is these binaries, and others like them, that currently characterise social actions and social exchanges that serve to undermine the development of cohesive societies in many parts of the world. Thus this Series is designed to provide support for policymakers, researchers and teachers who have responsibility to promote social harmony in their respective domains. It will help them with new thinking, new ideas and new directions to support the development of citizenship in the volatile times characterised by the 21st century.

Researchers interested in authoring or editing a book for this series are invited to contact the Series Publishing Editor: alice.xie@springernature.com.

All proposals will be reviewed by the Series Editors and editorial advisors.

Kerry J. Kennedy

Disruptions and Civic Education

How Should Young People be Prepared For an Uncertain Future?

Kerry J. Kennedy
Department of Curriculum and Instruction
The Education University of Hong Kong
Hong Kong, China

Department of Education and Curriculum
Studies
University of Johannesburg
Johannesburg, South Africa

ISSN 2211-1921　　　　　　　ISSN 2211-193X　(electronic)
SpringerBriefs in Education
ISSN 2524-8480　　　　　　　ISSN 2524-8499　(electronic)
SpringerBriefs in Citizenship Education for the 21st Century
ISBN 978-981-96-5874-9　　　ISBN 978-981-96-5875-6　(eBook)
https://doi.org/10.1007/978-981-96-5875-6

© The Editor(s) (if applicable) and The Author(s) 2025. This book is an open access publication.

Open Access This book is licensed under the terms of the Creative Commons Attribution-NonCommercial-NoDerivatives 4.0 International License (http://creativecommons.org/licenses/by-nc-nd/4.0/), which permits any noncommercial use, sharing, distribution and reproduction in any medium or format, as long as you give appropriate credit to the original author(s) and the source, provide a link to the Creative Commons license and indicate if you modified the licensed material. You do not have permission under this license to share adapted material derived from this book or parts of it.

The images or other third party material in this book are included in the book's Creative Commons license, unless indicated otherwise in a credit line to the material. If material is not included in the book's Creative Commons license and your intended use is not permitted by statutory regulation or exceeds the permitted use, you will need to obtain permission directly from the copyright holder.

This work is subject to copyright. All rights are solely and exclusively licensed by the Publisher, whether the whole or part of the material is concerned, specifically the rights of translation, reprinting, reuse of illustrations, recitation, broadcasting, reproduction on microfilms or in any other physical way, and transmission or information storage and retrieval, electronic adaptation, computer software, or by similar or dissimilar methodology now known or hereafter developed.

The use of general descriptive names, registered names, trademarks, service marks, etc. in this publication does not imply, even in the absence of a specific statement, that such names are exempt from the relevant protective laws and regulations and therefore free for general use.

The publisher, the authors and the editors are safe to assume that the advice and information in this book are believed to be true and accurate at the date of publication. Neither the publisher nor the authors or the editors give a warranty, expressed or implied, with respect to the material contained herein or for any errors or omissions that may have been made. The publisher remains neutral with regard to jurisdictional claims in published maps and institutional affiliations.

This Springer imprint is published by the registered company Springer Nature Singapore Pte Ltd.
The registered company address is: 152 Beach Road, #21-01/04 Gateway East, Singapore 189721, Singapore

If disposing of this product, please recycle the paper.

I would like to dedicate this book to the future and to the young people who need to bring us back from the brink. I think particularly of my grandchildren, Zoe, Jaime, Oliver, Henry, Annabel, Rose, Fletcher and Sam. The future is theirs. I hope that what is contained in this book might help them navigate new ways of confronting the disruptions that we currently experience and those ahead. It is only new thinking that can do this, new ways of being and new ways of constructing the future.
I would like to thank the Department of Curriculum and Instruction at The Education University of Hong Kong for supporting the development of this publication.

Contents

1 Twenty-First-Century Disruptions: Unpredictability as the New
  Normal 1
2 Preparing Young People for Disruptive Futures: How Can
  Education Contribute? 27
3 Shaping Education Futures: What Will Hinder and What Will
  Facilitate Change? 51
4 Civic Values for the Future: Constructing Communities
  of Well-Being 75
5 Life Education: Educating Citizens for Disruptive Futures 99

Chapter 1
Twenty-First-Century Disruptions: Unpredictability as the New Normal

Abstract 'Disruption' is a term that historically has been related to the world of business where it has meant drastic changes in processes of working or product development. In this chapter, and throughout this book, however, the term is used more broadly to describe economic upheavals caused by unemployment and technological innovation, atmospheric changes such as climate change and geopolitical disturbances such as war and terrorist actions. While these disruptions are described here one by one, the argument of this chapter is that very often in their effect they intersect with each other and with the social and political contexts in which they are embedded. There is also evidence that these multiple and intersecting disruptions influence different groups of people differently, with especially negative effects on the most vulnerable people across societies.

Keywords Disruption · Intersectionality · Contexts · Unpredictability

1.1 Introduction

Rotenstreich (1971) pointed to a key idea dominating Western intellectual thought at least since the nineteenth century, "the idea of progress (as) the controlling idea in the theory of history…a secular substitute for the earlier religious principle of Providence" (p. 1971). The appeal of the idea of civilizational progress, particularly Western civilization, is easy to understand, even though history itself tends to suggest that 'progress' has often been often costly. Colonial expansion, for example, once regarded as the great contribution of Western powers to global development, has subsequently been shown as inhumane, racist and exploitive (Said, 1993).

In a similar vein Allen (2017) argued that the work of philosophers such as Theodor Adorno and Michel Foucault, although coming from different starting points, nevertheless merged on a single idea: it should no longer be assumed that progress is the inevitable result of the historical development of civilizations. For Allen (2017), and indeed many other scholars, it has been argued that 'an end of progress' narrative is more characteristic of the present times.

© The Author(s) 2025
K. J. Kennedy, *Disruptions and Civic Education*,
SpringerBriefs in Citizenship Education for the 21st Century,
https://doi.org/10.1007/978-981-96-5875-6_1

Thus, when Simon and Tamm (2021) referred to "disconnected futures" (p. 7) divorced from the "scenarios of continuity" (p. 7), they were also endorsing 'the end of progress' narratives. According to these scenarios of continuity, the past and the present are always connected and there is progression from one to the other despite any intervening crises. In line with the main tenet of modernity, this view assumed control is always possible, vested entirely in the rationality of human thought. Yet changes related to such large-scale activities as the effects of climate change on the planet, the seemingly unstoppable advance of technologies and constant geopolitical conflict suggest that we are now in a period of "unimaginable futures" (p. 8) where nothing is predictable.

The theme of unpredictability in its multiple contexts will be explored in this chapter. This exploration will lay the foundations for considering increasing levels of unpredictability in further chapters and finally the implications for schools and the societies in which they are embedded.

Unpredictability takes many forms, and the focus here will be on those forms that intrude on people's lives in both direct and indirect ways. This will involve an examination of unpredictability in general, but particularly where it seems to characterize our current times. The following issues will form the basis of this examination:

- Disruption and unpredictability—meanings and implications
- Schumpeter's 'creative destruction'—the implications of economic disruption for individuals
- The Fourth Industrial Revolution (4IR) narrative—postmodern disruption
- Climate change—sceptics, activists and individuals
- Political disruption as a major feature of the twenty-first-century terrorism, political divides, dislocation and geopolitical tensions
- The intersection of these different disruptive forms and their potential impact on human life and activity.

1.2 Disruption—Meanings and Implications

Gans (2016) pointed out that "disruption is an overused term rendered almost useless as a conveyor of meaning" (p. 13). Yet the remainder of this book will be focused on it! The term is certainly used loosely. For example, Shane Goldmatcher (2024), writing in *The New York Times*, referred to President Donald Trump's "vision of vengeful disruption" being embraced by voters in the Iowa caucuses. Reuters (2024) referred to the "Red Sea disruption" as a result of Houthi attacks on passing vessels during the Israeli-Hamas war. Kim (2022) talked about "global supply chain disruption" as a result of the war in Ukraine. These everyday uses of the term suggest its basic meaning—to interrupt or intervene to bring about change. It may be political, war related, economic in nature or a myriad of other similar contexts. This may also extend to natural disasters such as earthquakes or tsunamis that are interventions of a different kind, but equally dramatic and at times equally devastating. These events share unpredictability. Yet these everyday constructions miss more technical meanings that are part of the history of the term.

Gans (2016) located the technical meaning of 'disruption' in the world of business. He defined it as "what a firm faces when the choices that once drove a firm's success now become those that destroy its future" (p. 13). He provided a case study showing how Blockbuster, a leading video rental company, was regarded as innovative and creative. Netflix came along with a similar product but ended with video streaming thus ending forever the video rental business. In this sense, video streaming was regarded as a 'disruptive' technology that challenged rentals and set the industry in a new direction. Yet Gans (2016) pointed out that while technology component was front and centre, "on a broader level (it was) an alternative business model for getting DVDs to consumers" (p. 18). The issue of technology and its role in disruption looms large in the literature and the point being made here is that disruption may not only be about technology. Other kinds of business practice may also signal the end of one way of doing business and the beginning of another. This issue will be discussed later in the next section.

It is possible to discuss 'disruption' as a theoretical construct, as has been done above. Yet whether as everyday occurrences or technical business processes, different kinds of disruptions have one thing in common: they are unpredictable and they impact on the lives of individuals in multiple ways. It might be the Houthis destroying shipping in the Red Sea or a company introducing new labour-saving technologies. One way or another these will both impact on lives, perhaps in at least one of these cases leading to death and in the other to job loss: for the individuals concerned both of these are devastating outcomes. They may be considered as separate and different.

Yet when different kinds of disruption mount up, especially in a short period of time, you end up with a book like Gordon Brown et al.'s (2023), *Permacrisis: A Plan to Fix a Fractured World*, that identified multiple global problems and posed potential solutions. We may not always call these disruptions, but it is their confluence that is important to understand, as it is with multiple disruptions. It is disruptions multiplying in the lives of individuals that are of most interest in this book. Whether they are technical or everyday disruptions, when they intersect their potential for impacting the lives of individuals multiplies, this issue will be explored throughout the remainder of this book. It will begin with what is described above as an example of 'technical' disruption or what might also be called a 'micro' disruption, impacting on both businesses and individuals.

1.3 Schumpeter's 'Creative Destruction'—The Implications of Economic Disruption for Individuals

Large-scale disruptions such as tsunamis, earthquakes, protests and revolutions will always grab the headlines. Yet there are other disruptions that are not so noticeable, even though their impact may be as significant as that of physical or social disruptions.

This is true of economic disruption designed to 'shake up' the economic system producing greater productivity and greater profits.

Schumpeter (1942) argued that "this process of Creative Destruction is the essential fact about capitalism" (p. 83). Sobel and Clements (2020) argued that other economists are more likely to argue that things like quality, price, location, etc., drive competition and therefore will determine winners and losers. This was not Schumpeter's view—economic change was more drastic, more dramatic, more consequential and more essential. He explained it this way (Schumpeter, 1942):

> The opening up of new markets, foreign or domestic, and the organizational development from the craft shop to such concerns as U.S. Steel illustrate the same process of industrial mutation—if I may use that biological term—that incessantly revolutionizes the economic structure from within, incessantly destroying the old one, incessantly creating a new one. (p. 83)

For Schumpeter, "capitalist reality is first and last a process of change" (p. 77). He spoke of the "gales of creative destruction" (pp. 81–86) that need to flow through firms to bring about change, increasing productivity and profits. In this scenario, 'creative destruction' was an essential element for the survival of capitalism. The status quo was not an option, staying the same was not an option, change was the only option if capitalism was to survive. "The gales of creative destruction" has become a *motif* flowing through a great deal of business literature seeking to explain how some firms survive, and others do not. An important question to address is what stimulates such change—how is 'creative destruction' actualized?

Alm and Cox (n.d.) argued that for Schumpeter "**e**ntrepreneurship and competition fuel creative destruction". Langlois (2002) showed that while the early Schumpeter focused on entrepreneurs as the catalysts for creative destruction many economists have argued that in his later work, he gave up this idea focusing instead on the effects of new forms of company management. Langlois (2002) contested this view arguing that Schumpeter maintained his commitment to the role of entrepreneurship, even though he recognized the changing nature of capitalism. Langlois's (2002) view was that "economic growth occurs at the hands of entrepreneurs, who bring into the system knowledge that is qualitatively new – knowledge not contained in the existing economic configuration" (pp. 15–16). It is the entrepreneur rather than the manager or even the owner who brings such knowledge to the firm or organization thus explaining the 'creative' side of 'creative destruction'. Schumpeter (1934) put it this way:

> What has been done already has the sharp-edged reality of all things which we have seen and experienced; the new is only the figment of our imagination. Carrying out a new plan and acting according to a customary one are things as different as making a road and walking along it. (p. 85)

At the heart of the work on entrepreneurs is the concept of innovation. It is economic innovation that is seen to drive economic progress. Without innovation there will only be stagnation—the same thing day after day. Innovation brings change and it is what the entrepreneur brings to the firm or organization. Without it there will be no change and without change, capitalism will be stifled.

Innovation can take many forms, but Rosenberg (2000) pointed to Schumpeter's view that "technological innovation is central to long term economic growth" (p. 11). This is consistent with Kaplinsky's (2011) view that Schumpeter was interested in "developing a theory of social and economic change in which technological development manifests itself as the most effective inner dynamics in social and economic change. It ... is only one of the factors, yet the most powerful factor on the way to change" (p. 4). The role of technology as a 'disruptor' has been subject to a great deal of analysis by business communities but there are now 'theories of disruption' suggesting that not all technological change may be 'disruptive'.

Such theories have reached some degree of sophistication. Christensen et al. (2015), for example, redefined disruptive technologies by arguing that they first target new markets with cut price products thus expanding the market and only subsequently challenging existing markets. In this framework, they argued that Uber was not a disruptive technology since it targeted traditional markets not new markets; but iPhone was new, because it challenged the monopoly computers had on access to the internet thus creating new markets at a lower cost. In the same vein, Skog et al. (2018) provided a new "conceptualization of how digital disruption may arise through embedding digital innovations that carry deviant value logics in digital ecosystems". In these cases, and others, the focus is on extending disruptive theory. This suggests a major concern in both business studies practice and literature with the 'creative' side of 'creative destruction'. Yet what about the 'destructive' side?

One way to look at this is simply to see how one technology replaces another: Ubers replace taxis, streaming replaces hard copy videos, online bookstores replace book shops, iPhones replace computers and ATMs replace bank tellers. Yet these examples emphasize the destruction of one product and the creation of new ones. This is by far the simplest war to view the destructive process, yet destruction goes way beyond the replacement of one product with another.

Arm and Cox (n.d.) pointed out that Schumpeter "coin (ed) the phrase 'technological unemployment'" and provided the following examples:

> E-mail, word processors, answering machines, and other modern office technology have cut the number of secretaries but raised the ranks of programmers. The birth of the Internet spawned a need for hundreds of thousands of webmasters, an occupation that did not exist as recently as 1990. LASIK surgery often lets consumers throw away their glasses, reducing visits to optometrists and opticians but increasing the need for ophthalmologists. Digital cameras translate to fewer photo clerks. (p. 4)

This is a fairly gentle description of the job losses that result from the 'destructive' side of 'creative destruction'. Some people lose jobs even though new ones are created. Alm and Cox (n.d.) described the necessity of this process as symptomatic of capitalism:

> A society cannot reap the rewards of creative destruction without accepting that some individuals might be worse off, not just in the short term, but perhaps forever. (p. 3)

For some economists, however, the trade-off—some jobs gone, others created, is not at all problematic. At the aggregate level often more jobs are created than lost and profits increase, and thus positive economic growth is the outcome despite job losses. Greenes (2003) described it like this:

> Merely counting the number of jobs destroyed in an industry without also taking account of the additional goods made possible by an innovation can be very misleading about the effects of economic changes. It confuses means(jobs) and ends (goods and services). For example, automatic dishwashers do the work that could have been done by workers using their hands. Is the destruction of hours of hand dishwashing jobs a tragedy? (p. 541)

At the aggregate level, the answer is obviously 'no'—the disappearance of low skilled jobs is not a tragedy. Yet at the individual level, the former dishwashers may well have regarded the loss of their jobs as a tragedy. Economists tend to assume that displaced workers will benefit from new jobs being created, although there is little evidence that this is the case. In this context, the effect of unemployment on individuals and their families, especially if they did not find new employment, is significantly underestimated.

This point is highlighted in an econometric study by Aghion et al. (2016) exploring the relationship between creative destruction and subjective well-being. They established that "the direct effects are that, everything else equal, more turnover translates into both, a higher probability of becoming unemployed for the employed which reduces life satisfaction, and a higher probability for the unemployed to find a new job, which increases life satisfaction" (p. 2). In subsequent analysis, they treat unemployment as a control variable, thus both acknowledging its effect and removing it. The issue here, as in the discussion of the previous study in the paragraph above, is whether there will be new jobs that will lead to higher levels of life satisfaction. If not, then the negative association between creative destruction and life satisfaction dominates the model. In such a model, it is of little use assuming that new job opportunities will always be available. This is the key issue to be discussed in the remainder of this section.

The effects of unemployment can be significant and should not be washed away in an econometric equation. While the economists' concerns for the aggregate rather than individual good are common, there are some who have investigated the impact of creative destruction on individuals. Huttunen et al. (2006), using labour market data from Norway, followed displaced workers over a seven-year period and found that:

> ...displacement significantly increases the probability of exiting the labor force. Workers who remain in the labor force suffer long-lasting negative earning losses.... Older workers, workers with low education levels and workers displaced from small plants are more vulnerable than other groups. Twenty percent of the displaced workers find a new job in a sister plant within the same firm. In the long run, 35 percent of the displaced workers change industry, as compared to 17 percent of nondisplaced workers.

This is a more realistic picture of the 'destructive' side of creative destruction since it considers the impact on individuals rather than just any aggregate good created. Further, Komlos (2014) argued that earlier disruptions, such as the introduction of the steam engine, automobiles and electricity, generated relatively small destructive after-effects and very large aggregate benefits. Yet with current disruptions "our conjecture is that the benefits reaped from creative destruction has declined substantially over time and is likely to remain at a low level" (p. 7). An example is instructive:

> …the smartphone replaced simple cell phones and traditional cameras. The "selfie" replaced the "Kodak moment" but Kodak employed 86,000 in 1998, and 145,000 at its peak (and paid them mostly middle-class wages), while in 2014, after emerging from bankruptcy, it has a skeleton workforce of 8,000. (pp. 7–8)

Komlos (2014) concluded on a sober note:

> The new technologies might well be brilliant and create immense wealth for a few, thereby continuing to exacerbate socio-economic inequality and exclude an ever increasing share of the population from the middle class. Yet, the numbers of underemployed and working poor will probably swell… It is more than likely that we have entered an age of a new normal… that will resemble more closely the social structure of the *ancien regime* than that of an ephemeral ideal economy. (p. 15)

In conclusion, this section has explored the concept of 'creative destruction' as developed by the economist, Joseph Schumpeter. Originally designed to explain the need for constant change in the capitalist economic system, the focus has more often been on the 'creative' side. This includes the development of new products or processes or ideas that replace those existing and lead to new markets or the shifting of markets from the old product to the new. The downside of this creativity is that it inevitably leads to destruction of some kind—the old product, the existing workforce, the way the market is configured, etc. For some economists, the aggregate good produced by the new product, process, etc., outweighs any negative effects of the destructive element. Yet others have shown at the individual level that destruction can be devastating. At the same time, more recently the contribution of the new product to aggregate good may be minimal. This is the main point to understand in this section—individual lives can be affected by economic change in ways that are unaccounted for by traditional economics. Yet for individuals, their families and their communities, the destructive elements of economic change need to be understood and monitored. They represent one set of disruptions, but they are not the only ones as will be shown in the other chapters of this book. Initially, however, the focus will be on current new ways of promoting both creativity and destruction in the lives of individuals.

1.4 Postmodern 'Disruption'—The Fourth Industrial Revolution (4IR) and Its Narratives

Very often when examples of 'disruption' are provided, the focus is on the past such, as the steam engine, the automobile or the computer. Yet in talking about the Fourth Industrial Revolution (4IR), Klaus Schwab (2016) referred to 'disruption' over forty times as characteristic of 4IR. Other writers have referred to terms used specifically by Schumpeter such as 'creative destruction' (Nizami, 2019) or "technological unemployment" (Peters, 2017), both referring to the effects of 4IR. Yet others link Schumpeter's work in economic growth theory and 4IR (Kop, 2022; Venturini, 2022).

The links drawn between Schumpeterian economics and 4IR suggest a linear and largely unproblematic relationship that is not atypical of economic thinking. Yet from a social perspective, issues of 4IR are far from unproblematic, to the point where for some there is not even agreement that 4IR exists. Yet there are also other more nuanced understandings, and it is helpful to understand them and their constructions of 4IR.

1.4.1 Discourses Constructing 4IR

There is a wealth of 4IR literature addressing issues of theory, policy and practice including some to which I have contributed (Kennedy, 2023). All of it refers in one way or another to the role of technology in future economic development. Not all of it, however, speaks with a single voice. Originally, I distinguished two discourses—realist and imaginary (Kennedy, 2023). Based on the literature, however, I have taken an expanded view identifying technological advocates, dissenters and others in between. These provide important perspectives on both the nature of 4IR and the social contexts that have constructed it and its implications for the future.

1.4.2 'Techno-Realist'—Advocating the Creative Side of 4IR

A good starting point for understanding an advocate's view of 4IR is with the work of Klaus Schwab, the founder and Director of the World Economic Forum (WEF). When participants arrived for the WEF in 2016, they were given Schwab's (2016) book, *The Fourth Industrial Revolution*, that also happened to be the theme for that year's WEF. Written now almost a decade ago, the book assumes the reality of 4IR, but also pays attention to its implications.

Technology is at the centre of Schwab's narrative, but it is not so much about pieces of technology like computers, the internet or handphones. Rather, it is about integrated systems of technology (Schwab, 2016):

> artificial intelligence (AI), robotics, the internet of things (IoT), autonomous vehicles, 3D printing, nanotechnology, biotechnology, materials science, energy storage and quantum computing, to name a few. Many of these innovations are in their infancy, but they are already reaching an inflection point in their development as they build on and amplify each other in a fusion of technologies across the physical, digital and biological worlds. (p. 7)

Using historical comparisons with what he called the first, second and third industrial revolutions, he characterizes and differentiates 4IR by the speed with which technologies are developing, the extent of their influence and the impact ranging from within single industries to whole societies (pp. 8–9). He is clearly a technology advocate, and, on that basis, I originally classified him as a 'realist' (Kennedy, 2023). Yet he is not an unthinking technological optimist. I think his work is more nuanced.

Schwab seems to fit better into a category called the "techno-realist", defined as (Technorealism, 2021):

> Technorealism demands that we think critically about the role that tools and interfaces play in human evolution and everyday life. Integral to this perspective is our understanding that the current tide of technological transformation, while important and powerful, is actually a continuation of waves of change that have taken place throughout history.

After Schwab analyses the new technologies characteristic of 4IR, he acknowledges their impact including the possibility of significant unemployment, the disappearance of existing industries, increasing inequality and the need for people to control technology and its uses. From the beginning, he acknowledged that "the more we think about how to harness the technology revolution, the more we will examine ourselves and the underlying social models that these technologies embody and enable, and the more we will have an opportunity to shape the revolution in a manner that improves the state of the world" (p. 9). He does not give up on supporting new technologies, but with his reflective-like stance he understands contexts and their potential impact on the lives of individuals. This makes him a techno-realist rather than a simple realist or techno-optimist.

1.4.3 Techno-Dissenters and 4IR Pessimism

Technorealism is by no means a radical position. Yet such a stance, as measured as it may seem, is not acceptable to all. There are critics of 4IR who might be described as "techno-pessimists", in contrast with Schwab's technorealism. Such a term, however, seems inadequate for the critique launched by Moll (2022). It is perhaps better to describe him as a "4IR pessimist", since he sought to undermine the entire idea of a "fourth industrial revolution". For him, the new technologies, the resulting unemployment, the consistent offshoring of low-level work, etc., are simply extensions of the third industrial revolution (3IR). Throughout his paper, there is little disagreement with Schwab on the statistics or the trends. The disagreement is over the labelling of them as 'the fourth industrial revolution'. This is an economist's argument about where the line can be drawn between 3 and 4IR, but it does not change the pace of technological change. Yet Moll (2022) raised a crucial point referring to what he sees as 3IR—but it is equally relevant to 4IR:

> The realities of the world are still those of the 3IR, and not much change is in sight. These realities are about globalization, and the tensions between those who drive it and benefit from it. (p. 54)

The idea of both 'winners' and 'losers' from 4IR is not well addressed by techno-realists such as Schwab. Moll (2022) drew on Manuel Castells to support his view:

> ...globally 3IR geopolitical patterns of the marginalization of the South continue, whether by continued offshoring, or onshoring back to automated factories, or simply by discarding the "people (or places [mostly the poorer countries of Africa]) who are not, or are not any longer, considered valuable, even if they are still physically there" (Castells, 1999, p. 9). All the evidence of offshoring and foreign outsourcing suggests a deepening of the exploitative patterns of the 3IR. (p. 53)

Understanding these "exploitive patterns" is important whether they are attributed to 4IR or 3IR. One way to understand was provided Moll by (2021). He linked Schwab's 4IR discourse to neoliberalism that highlights 'trickle down' economics. van Kesteren et al. (2019) expanded on this idea:

> Trickle down policies favour (large) companies and rich people through tax facilities and investments, assuming that the positive effects will also 'seep down' to the poor at the bottom of the pyramid.

Moll (2022) provided an example of the trickle-down effect referring to workers in an Indian sweat shop exploited by an economic system that sent low levels tasks offshore. It was his additional comment, however, that highlighted the actual "trickle down" when he added, "these wages are no doubt welcome in impoverished families" (p. 53), and undoubtedly, they were. Yet as Stiglitz (2016) put it, the assumption of neoliberalism and much economic policy of the twenty-first century was that "resources given to the rich would inevitably 'trickle down' to the rest".

Is this also the case with 4IR? Will it benefit only the rich in the Global North at the expense of the Global South where disruptions can be expected to hit very hard? While Schwab does not address this question, others do (Kaisara et al., 2021). We need to keep in mind that the unequal distribution of disruptions will affect some more than others with, in some case, catastrophic effects. The contribution of Moll (2022), a clear "techno-dissenter", is to have highlighted this issue. It is a neglected but significant outcome of the likely technology disruptions among those who benefit little from them and it contrasts with Schwab's constantly upbeat projection. Some will win—but others will lose.

1.4.3.1 4IR as a Techno/Social Imaginary

In addition to the techno-realists and pessimists, there is a final construction of 4IR to consider: 4IR as a 'social imaginary'. The concept of 'social imaginary' has a relatively long history in sociology (Taylor, 2004) and has been subject to a good deal of review and analysis (James, 2019). The latter defined 'imaginary' in the following way:

> In common use, the concept of 'the imaginary' came to refer to something invented or not real, something projected into the future, imagined beyond itself… even this imaginary projection of invented possibilities has to have a place to stand, a place from which to project imaginations. We do not imagine out of nothing. And, therefore, the imaginary provides one locus to begin to understand the complexity of human being. (p. 37)

This does not mean the 'imaginary' is necessarily untrue, but often those doing the imagining are elites (Taylor, 2004) creating the world as they would like to see it. Schiølin (2020) pointed out that imaginaries are also about power since they seek to shape and determine the future. Schwab (2016), of course, speaks of 4IR in realist terms and would not accept that he has created an "imaginary" in the sense discussed here or that he is concerned simply with power. Yet as shown above there are those who question the very existence of 4IR (Moll, 2022). Thus, thinking about 4IR in a less deterministic sense and more as scenario of possibility makes some sense. Such a stance means we can be more reflective about Schwab's (2016) vision, more able to interrogate it in our different contexts and better able to make use of its underpinning ideas where they are relevant.

However we theorize about or seek to conceptualize our current times, we can be sure at the very least of the practices that make up those times: new technologies, increasing use of AI, replacement of humans with machines and, of course, disruptions that result from all of these. It is these practices that we need to take note of when it comes to considering both their effects and appropriate responses to them.

1.5 Climate Change-Disruption as a Survival Strategy

If 4IR has attracted a great deal of publicity and attention in this century, it has been matched by discourses related to climate change. Yet it may be that 'change' is a euphemism since increasingly there are references to the 'disruptions' caused by such change. In response to the physical disruptions caused by climate change, there have also social disruptions. These have been largely in support of more aggressive policies to combat what are seen as the inevitability of climate change and the reluctance of governments to address the issues. Finally, and perhaps most importantly, in addition to ongoing discourses on climate change and disruption and social disruptions about the lack of climate change policies, there is the effect of climate change on the lives of individuals. These multiple aspects of climate change and their interaction will be highlighted in what follows.

1.5.1 Climate Change or Climate Disruption?

When it comes to climate change, Woodward (2019) identified what I would call 'double disruptions':

> Just as climate change results from disrupted Earth systems, the response to climate change will disrupt established patterns of energy use, transport, economic transactions, building design, and health care. (p. 45)

The first of these as shown here might be summarized as disruptions to the climate on account of radical and seemingly unexplained causes while the second are social disruptions the results of which will be the subject of politics and policies. It is helpful to see these two ends of the spectrum—unexplained causes and social responses. Yet there is an important issue to clarify.

The "disrupted Earth systems" do not become so of their own accord. Woodward (2019) was clear that "there are particular features of observed climate change that identify, unambiguously, the influence of human activity" (p. 44). Yet he provided minimal evidence. Crowly (2000), on the other hand, examined different aspects of climate change over the past 1000 years, coming down on the side of human rather than natural causes. Stern and Kaufman (2014) were in general agreement with this analysis, although with minor reservations in some areas. The scientific conclusion that "disrupted Earth systems" are caused largely by human-environment interactions seems neither surprising nor, given the complexity of the science, contestable. Yet the reception of this explanation in the community has created sceptics, climate sceptics, who do not just dispute the conclusion but the very nature of climate science.

Tranter and Booth (2015) showed there is little consistency when it comes to identifying climate change sceptics. There are variations both within and across countries relating to gender, education and attitudes to the environment. The highest level of scepticism seems to be in Western countries such as the United States, Australia and the United Kingdom. Sceptics do not necessarily have negative attitudes to the environment. Most often they simply disagree with the climate science. Education does not always lead to a more enlightened attitude to the views of climate scientists. These results suggest that climate sceptics do not fit a neat pattern of potential conspiracy theorists. Yet their protests, often loud and very public, potentially undermine scientific explanations for climate change. Perhaps more importantly, such protests can impede the social solutions needed to prevent further disruption. There is thus a link between scientific and social aspects of climate change—if there are those who do not believe the science it is unlikely they will support the need for change. This has become a major issue that will be discussed in the following section.

1.5.2 Disruptions Focusing on the Urgency of Social Change Policies

Climate change sceptics disbelieve the science and become sceptical of the need for broad social changes that can help to relieve the disruption. Yet there are others who believe the science and are impatient because there is inadequate social change. One outcome of the latter has been characterized as "youth activism on climate change" (O'Brien et al., 2018). Such activism is not necessarily in direct opposition to the climate sceptics, but rather within "a political climate that is marked by powerful interests, strong rhetoric, and weak action on climate change" (p. 42). Often the opposition is seen to be governments slow on policy development, too responsive to pressure groups and overly aware of the costs of transitioning an economy from reliance on such things as fossil fuels and carbon emissions. For young people, the issue is not about navigating sensitive policy development or needing to remain in office: it is about their future and the kind of life they see for themselves as part of that future. Selfish? Possibly. But controlling the future appears to be a key issue for young people aware that in general they do not have power over themselves or their future. This lack of power appears to be enough motivation for political engagement on the climate change issue.

Despite the mobilization of youth supporting climate change action, evidence that it has been effective in bringing about the desired changes is rare (Han & Ahn, 2020). Yet in different countries it has certainly made its point especially by causing considerable social disruption. Axon (2019), for example, discussed the case of Extinction Rebellion in England:

> Extinction Rebellion protesters participate in resistance that causes active disruption to everyday life to others that are continuing with unsustainable overconsumption. This level of action can be related to Foucauldian notions of resistance. (p. 14)

As the BBC (2018) coverage of these protests pointed out, "they've blocked bridges, glued themselves to the gates of Downing Street, and closed roads, all in the name of stopping climate change". This is an intermediate form of social disruption designed to force the hand of governments, industry and other elites to act more quickly and with greater focus for the cause of climate justice. In other words, from the young protesters' perspective, the major social disruptions needed to attenuate the effects of climate change can only be achieved through intermediate forms of disruption designed to shock people out of their complacency. There is a certain quixotism about this approach. It is perhaps related to the idealism so often associated with young people, possibly reflecting the limited range of tools available to those without access to power.

Yet it should also be pointed out that this overt form of protest behaviour does not characterize every from of youth climate action. O'Brien et al. (2018) identified three distinct forms of youth climate action: "dutiful dissent", "disruptive dissent" and "dangerous dissent". These move from working well within the system to bring about change to challenging key groups and interests in order to promote radical change. The important point about the latter two categories is that while they may use overt or unconventional forms of protest, as in the case of the Extinction Rebellion example, their interests are more about ideas and challenging the system. The tools they choose to use should not be mistaken for the focus of their protests: tools are always a means to a greater end that is best summarized as climate justice. Such justice is not an abstract concept—it is about saving individuals impacted by climate disruption as will be shown in the following section.

1.5.3 Climate Disruption and Individual Lives

There is a tendency in climate change discourses towards abstraction around purposes and preferred futures. Yet in the end it is individuals who are at the end of climate disruptions, individuals who will experience impacts from different sources, some of which will be direct while others will be indirect. Distinguishing effects in this way provides insights into the nature and extent of climate change.

1.5.3.1 Direct Effects

There are well-known direct effects: changing ocean levels threatening life in island nations, especially in the Pacific (Kiribati, Vanuatu, Tuvalu, Solomon Islands, Samoa, Nauru and Fiji), raging bushfires across continents threatening homes and lives, and floods that turn people out of their homes. Less well known are pressures from climate leading to psychological conditions (Burke et al., 2018), mental stress (Clayton, 2020) and more general health conditions (Al-Delaimy et al., 2020). The extent of these different direct effects is not well known and certainly is not fully documented. Yet it does seem that whatever the extent, the psychological impact of climate change is not evenly distributed with the poor and disadvantaged suffering the most.

Islam and Winkel (2017) argued that there were three main reasons the poor suffer from climate disruptions more than the rich:

- increase in the exposure to climate hazards;
- increase in the susceptibility to damage caused by climate hazards; and
- decrease in the ability to cope with and recover from the damage.

While their analysis is focused largely on individuals, they also argue that low-income countries are more exposed to climate disruptions than high-income countries. They provided only anecdotal evidence for their claim but conceptually they make a strong case about the vulnerability of those who lack resources of different kinds. Nevertheless, their conclusions are consistent with other research that raises the issues of climate vulnerability among disadvantaged groups (Klinenberg et al., 2020; Thomas et al., 2019). A general conclusion from this line of research is that multidisciplinary approaches are needed to understand the nature of climate change and its impact. Climate science itself is largely based on the physical and biological sciences. But climate justice needs to take advantage of what the social sciences have to offer, especially when it comes to considering the impact on individual lives.

1.5.3.2 Indirect Effects of Climate Disruptions

There is an extensive literature documenting what can be called the indirect effects of climate disruption. These involve biophysical changes in the environment that have the potential to affect flora and fauna, the economy, health, homes and even entire cities (Myers & Bernstein, 2011). These latter are directly affected, but they then act as mediators to go on and affect people as well. As with direct effects, the most impact from indirect effects will likely be felt by disadvantaged groups and communities. Amorim-Maia et al. (2022) developed a model to try and address the equity issues associated with climate change disruption.

The entirety of the model is complex, but one aspect of it recommends itself because it highlights one of the key issues: the need for communication on climate change issues. It comes under the general heading of "promot(ing) cross-identity and -vulnerability climate action and community resilience building" (p. 12). At the heart of the recommendation is the need to empower vulnerable communities. This can be done by informing them on a regular basis about changes needed at the community level on account of climate change and advising on actions that can be taken. This moves the nature of community engagement from one involving consultation by authorities to one involving action on the part of vulnerable communities. Yet this will only work if there is a flow of information and if resources are made available to support whatever action is needed. At the same time, this needs to be more than a neoliberal solution placing responsibility on individuals: governments need to realize that such solutions require support and encouragement if vulnerable communities are to become active agents in responding to climate disruptions.

1.6 Political Disruptions—A Twenty-First-Century Phenomenon?

Referring to World War I, the author, H. G. Wells, coined the phrase, "the war to end wars". Speaking to the US Congress in 1917, President Woodrow Wilson described the purpose of that war as "making the world safe for democracy". Yet just over a decade later, Adolf Hitler was rising to power in Germany and another war was being planned war. At about the same time militarism was in full swing in Japan and within years the country launched its attack on China as a prelude to another major war in Asia. World War II was followed by post-colonial independence movements across Asia and Africa, then wars in Korea, then Vietnam and eventually over Kuwait to prevent the Iraqi aggression.

An overlay on this activity was a 'cold war' with the United States and the Union of Soviet Socialist Republics as the respective leaders of the opposing forces. Ronald Reagan's "tear down the wall, Mr Gorbachev" speech in 1987 was an attempt to undermine the Soviet Empire. Yet by the late 1980s the USSR was in such disarray that it only required a gentle shove to push it over. This led one political scientist to declare "the end of history" and the triumph of liberal democracy (Fukuyama, 1989). Yet the final two years of the century involved ethnic conflict in Eastern Europe between Serbian Christians and Albanian Muslims. Condemned by the United Nations for its violence, a NATO bombing campaign in 1999 brought the conflict to an end. The twentieth century ended much as it had begun: characterized by war, violence and hatred.

How, then, can the twenty-first century be characterized?

It is tempting to see the new century as a continuation of the old. The destruction of the World Trade Center in New York on 11 September 2001 by jihadi terrorists was the first major disruption of the twenty-first century. Yet it was remarkably different from the clashes between nation states in the twentieth century. Those responsible were non-state actors motivated by an extremist view of their religion and a mission to—or perhaps against—the world. The optimism of the twenty-first century was shattered by these events that are commemorated in the 9/11 Memorial and Museum in New York where it is possible to relive the dreadful terror of the day and its aftermath. The then President, George Bush (2001) provided an image of the attack that is likely printed into the minds of many Americans:

> The pictures of airplanes flying into buildings, fires burning, hugh structures collapsing, have filled us with disbelief, terrible sadness, and a quiet, unyielding anger. These acts of mass murder were intended to frighten our nation into chaos and retreat. But they have failed; our country is strong.

Following the destruction of the World Trade Centre, *The New York Times* commented (Tharoor, 2001):

> ... the twenty-first century will be the century of "one world" as never before, with a consciousness that the tragedies of our time are all global in origin and reach, and that tackling them is also a global responsibility that must be assumed by us all. Interdependence is now the watchword.

This statement was in one sense a reflection of the globalization discourse that had dominated political and economic discussions in the 1990s. Yet it was also a recognition that a combination of advanced technology and ideology had already proven to be a powerful twenty-first-century weapon. At the same time, it was also a plea to avoid a retreat into isolationism. Subsequent US-led wars in Afghanistan and Iraq showed that in the immediate years after the destruction of the World Trade Center US policymakers, both Republican and Democratic took their global role seriously. But it was at great cost, as pointed out by Savell (2023). In a major report for Brown University's Watson Institute for International and Public, she estimated that:

> The total death toll in the post-9/11 war zones of Afghanistan, Pakistan, Iraq, Syria, and Yemen could be at least 4.5-4.7 million.... Some of these people were killed in the fighting, but far more, especially children, have been killed by the reverberating effects of war, such as the spread of disease. These latter indirect deaths – estimated at 3.6-3.8 million – and related health problems have resulted from the post-9/11 wars' destruction of economies, public services, and the environment. Indirect deaths grow in scale over time.

The key point highlighted here is that wars involve not only participants (referred to as the direct effects) but also the "collapse of economies, including food insecurity, the decline in provision of public services and infrastructure, including health services, contamination of the environment and ongoing trauma and violence", referred to as indirect effects (Savell, 2023). Thus, the disruption represented by the attack on the World Trade Center cascaded into multiple disruptions for the individuals represented by the toll of the subsequent wars. The former has achieved great attention in the public consciousness, the latter less so, despite its extent. Yet it is important to recognize that while the original attack was horrendous, so too was its aftermath. Disruptions such as these are a reminder of how toxic human interactions can become when ideology drives actions.

1.6 Political Disruptions—A Twenty-First-Century Phenomenon?

If 9/11 initiated disruptions in the twenty-first century, they have only been a beginning. Apart from what might be called the "9/11 wars" referred to above there have been others, the most important of which are still ongoing at the time of writing. There are major unresolved have been major conflicts in Myanmar and Sudan that have wrought untold damage on the local population. At the same time, Russia's unprovoked attack on Ukraine, lasting now for over two years, and Israel's response to an attack by Hamas leading to the devastation of Gaza and assaults on Lebanon and Syria share several similarities.

The first is their ideology-driven motivations. Russia's war was provoked by ultra-nationalism and irredentism that ignored entirely the late history of the twentieth century. Rather, Russian ideologues reconstructed history to promote the idea of a 'Greater Russia' made up of past history and ideas. Ukraine is the first step in building this Greater Russia. As for Hamas, from its beginning, it "call(ed) for the destruction of Israel and the establishment of an Islamic society in historic Palestine" (Robinson, 2023). Its direct attack on Israel in October 2023 was an outcome of this ideology that has fuelled Israeli-Palestinian relations for some time. These twenty-first-century wars have shown that ideologies of different kinds have become a hallmark of the century. In the twentieth century at the end of the Cold War it seems that conflicting ideologies had been overcome. But in the twenty-first century new ideologies surfaced, and many would argue they have created a more polarized world partly influenced by religion (in Russia, for example, ultra-nationalism has been encouraged and supported by the Orthodox Church) and Hamas' objectives make the central role of religion clear. Huntington (2011) once talked about the "clash of civilizations" as a way to understand global politics at the end of the Cold War. While it is a highly contested view, there is little doubt that much of what has happened since his book first appeared can be framed in this way. Yet to think only in these terms misses an important point: the impact of ongoing conflicts hits mainly at individuals and their families. That is, geopolitical disruptions continue to have a disproportionate impact on those who have done little to bring about the conflicts in the first place.

There are no official lists of either military or civilian deaths because of the Russian-Ukraine War. Estimates differ considerably but one thing is clear: daily television footage in living rooms across the globe attests to the personal devastation brought to the Ukrainian people. This does not need any 'official' authentication. Military deaths are another question but whatever they are—80,000, 90,000 or 100,000 on each side—it is an immoral figure. The same can be said for Gaza—journalists and television reports show us the chaos, the devastation and the annihilation of a civilization. Similar carnage can also be seen in Lebanon. Women, children and hospital patients are neither immune nor protected from the Israeli Defences Force seeking, in the words of the Israeli Prime Minister Netanyahu, 'to destroy Hamas' and more recently Hezbollah. It is unlikely that civilians in either Ukraine or Gaza initiated military conflict, but they bear much of the brunt of the destruction and killing. War is a major political disruption, but it is even a greater disruption for civilian populations at the mercy of armies, drones and rockets and with little means of defence. This is the downside of global engagement, but global withdrawal can be equally problematic.

Global withdrawal in relation to foreign policy is often referred to as isolationism—a deliberate strategy on the part of nation states to refrain from interacting or engaging with other countries. While the positive side of this may avoid the tragedies of Ukraine and Gaza, Zappone (2024) pointed to the negative side. He cited the election of Donald Trump as President of the United States in 2016:

> … this marked the mainstreaming of populism, it exposed the peril of disinformation, and made the backlash against globalisation real – in short, the election sparked the crisis in liberal democracy that has defined our time. Today, authoritarian regimes, often by subversive means, seek to reshape the international order.

Cox (2018) argued that populism in the twenty-first century is a global rather than national phenomenon. It is exemplified by Trump's "America First", Nigel Farage's 'Brexit', Hungary's Victor Orban with his "Stop Brussels" campaign and Poland's Law and Justice Party's narrative of "Poland in ruins". While these are scattered national initiatives with very little formal collaboration between them, they send a strong message: the nation state has risen to challenge a globalized world, the nation state needs to be protected, especially those within it who are said to be the victims of globalization, strangers and foreigners are not welcome and elites are not trusted. All of this leads to highly polarized societies where groups are pitted against each other as the nation state itself isolates from the world. All the populists above use the tolls of democracy such as elections for their own purposes, but they are not committed to the full range of democratic values.

Coupled with the rises of populism in the twenty-first century has been the constant development of new technologies. This has meant information has become perhaps the most contested commodity on the globe. 'Misinformation', 'disinformation', 'fake news' and multiple ways of distorting information carried directly to mobile phones and other individualized devices. Deep fake videos falsifying people's images and words, artificial intelligence (AI) portraying fake voices, chat bots pretending to be human and conveying false information. Information superhighways stretching from one end of the globe to the other meant there were no barriers to different forms of fake information crossing borders. This combination of politics and fake news was not just a new political form: rather, it became a powerful and disruptive force in the lives of individuals.

Bennet and Livingston (2018) distinguished between fake news that "tends to frame the problem as isolated incidents of falsehood and confusion" (p. 124) and disinformation that "invites looking at more systematic disruptions of authoritative information flows due to strategic deceptions that may appear very credible to those consuming them" (p. 124). While this is an interesting distinction, the issue for individuals is that different kinds of false information arrive indiscriminately to mislead and confuse with limited means available to disentangle true from false. There is a growing literature suggesting that this confusing context can affect mental well-being, create negative emotions and lead to social instability (Claudia, 2022; Nela & Parruca, 2023). What starts as political ends up as personal, affecting both young people and adults.

What is more, it affects some young people more than other. Using PISA data, Suarez-Alvarez (2021) showed that in every participating country students from disadvantaged backgrounds were not as well equipped with strategies to "assess the credibility of sources" (p. 3) as students from advantaged backgrounds. This suggests that low SES students are more likely to be impacted by fake news and disinformation simply because they have fewer strategies to resist. In addition, a number of studies has shown that support for populism is more likely to come from people, and particularly from men, categorized as having both low levels of education and lower socio-economic status (Anduiza et al., 2019; Gidron & Hall, 2017; Gradstein, 2024). This is a double blow to the working class disrupted by populist political narratives as well the technologies that support their widespread dissemination. It is this issue of multiple disruptions and their impact on the lives of individuals that will be taken up in the next section.

The intersection of multiple disruptive forms and their potential impact on human life and activity.

Throughout this chapter, disruptions have been referred to as singular events, but what if they do not act as such in the lives of individuals? Intersectionality theory offers a way to conceptualize the possibility of multiple impacts resulting from disruptions (Grzanka, 2020):

> …unlike a causal or explanatory proposition that can be falsified, intersectionality is more aptly characterized as a lens or a frame…. if we consider single-axis, demographic/identitarian, variable-centered approaches to represent the epistemic riptide… of canonical social science… then intersectionality is an epistemic shift toward rendering social-psychological experiences in person-centered relief. (p. 7)

The idea of intersectionality being described here is that it focuses on the actual experience of individuals rather than assuming that experience can be understood from a process that highlights average effects. Statisticians refer to this as difference between person-centred analyses and variable-centred analyses. The former enable the identification of individuals with similar dispositions or characteristics. Often these analyses show that individuals can be classified by multiple characteristics. For example, Chow and Kennedy (2014) showed that in trying to account for participation in unconventional forms of civic engagement (e.g., street protest) gender, class and level of civic knowledge were the best indicators of such participation. Working-class boys with low levels of civic knowledge were more likely than others to participate in protest activities. There is not a causal link between these indicators and participation in such activities, but there is a likelihood that these indicators play an important role. This is the essence of person-centred analysis—it is indicative rather than prescriptive.

Grzanka (2020) provided a perspective on intersectionality from the point of view of psychology. Sociologists have also taken an interest in intersectionality research. Collins and Chepp (2013) provided what has become a standard sociological definition of intersectionality:

> Intersectionality consists of an assemblage of ideas and practices that maintain that gender, race, class, sexuality, age, ethnicity, ability, and similar phenomena cannot be analytically

understood in isolation from one another; instead, these constructs signal an intersecting constellation of power relationships that produce unequal material realities and distinctive social experiences for individuals and groups positioned within them. (p. 58)

The essence of this definition is the basic sociological constructs of power and equality: disadvantaged groups and individuals are always at the wrong end of these constructs being without power and unequal in relation to their oppressors. An intersectional approach highlights is that for some people lack power and inequality are exacerbated. Differences between students such as race, class gender, ethnicity and sexuality are not in themselves forms of disadvantage—indeed, the opposite should be the case. Yet in social contexts difference can become disadvantage as Kennedy and Henderson (2024) pointed out with reference to Australia:

…First Nations students have the lowest participation rate in senior secondary schooling of any group in the community; some women continue to face difficulties in gaining access to highly paid occupations; some Australians from non-English-speaking backgrounds have difficulty gaining access to the labour market, except at the lowest paid levels; and people with intellectual and physical disabilities cannot always gain access to mainstream education and employment. In most cases, these barriers are not an infringement of the legal structures that support equality and anti-discrimination. Rather, they are socially constructed practices that derive from practices in society and are real in the lives of different individuals. (p. 65)

Imagine from the above quote there is a young woman from a non-English-speaking background who lives with her parents whose incomes are below the poverty line. Rizvi (1993) referred to such a situation as one of "intersecting disadvantage". It is not known how such disadvantage operates, but that it does so is clear from many cases not only in Australia, but globally.

The issue to understand now is how does intersectionality as described above influence our understanding of disruptions and their impact in the lives of Individuals.

1.6.1 Intersecting Disruptions

Intersectionality offers a process that highlights multiplicities, interactions and influences that cannot always be explained. As with the original conception of intersectionality (Crenshaw, 1989), there is a touch of poststructuralism in the concept's development and therefore lack of any specific understanding of cause and effect. Yet complex social actions can rarely be simply explained. Intersectionality highlights this point and suggests that we may gain more insight to the impact of disruptions if we recognize the complexities and the possibilities of interaction leading to effects.

Steinfield et al. (2021) developed the "cross-scale intersectionality matrix (CSIM) to better understand the differing impacts of environmental disruptions and envisage effective solutions". A graphic representation of the model can be found in the article (p. 261) and also here: https://www.researchgate.net/figure/The-Cross-Scale-Intersectionality-Matrix-CSIM_fig1_346503780.

At the centre of CSIM are multiple environmental disruptions that take many forms: "droughts, typhoons, earthquakes, fires, tsunamis, erratic rainfalls, floods, mudslides, (plastic) pollution, oil or toxic spills, and resource depletions" (Steinfield et al., 2021, p. 263). These are devastating enough in themselves, but there are also intersections of these kind of disruption with their social, economic and political contexts. Environmental disruptions intersect with the lives of individuals, but they do not influence everyone in the same way. Women, working-class families, and people with special needs will suffer more than others. Impacts may be in terms of livelihood or food security or labour market engagement. All of this takes place within macro geopolitical and social contexts. There are multiple interactions within CSIM, and in strictly scientific terms, it is impossible to attribute cause and effect. Yet what is clear is that environmental disruptions are not single or isolated events: other disruptions follow affecting not only the environment but also the lives of individuals.

Disruptions cannot be studied as individual events: they are interactive and intersectional. They occur in different contexts and both influence and are influenced by those contexts. It is these broad contexts that are important to understand since without the understanding of intersecting disruptions and the effect they have on individuals any understanding will be limited. The challenges posed by disruptions cannot be met serially but the challenges can be met if they properly understand. This is the role of education that can prepare young people to confront and navigate disruption. The following chapter will explore education's potential for doing this as well as the barriers that all too often constrain education's potential.

References

Aghion, P., Akcigit, U., Deaton, A., & Roulet, A. (2016). Creative destruction and subjective well-being. *American Economic Review, 106*(12), 3869–3897.
Al-Delaimy, W., Ramanathan, V., & Sorondo, M. (Eds.). (2020). *Health of people, health of planet and our responsibility—Climate change, air pollution and health*. Springer.
Allen. A. (2017). Adorno, Foucault, and the end of progress: Critical theory in postcolonial times. In In C. Lafont & P. Deutscher (Eds.), *Critical theory in critical times: Transforming the global political and economic order* (pp. 183–206). Columbia University Press.
Alm & Cox. (n.d.). *Creative destruction* (pp. 1–11). Accessed on 24 January 2024 from https://www.econlib.org/library/Enc/CreativeDestruction.html
Anduiza, E., Guinjoan, M., & Roco, G. (2019). Populism, participation, and political equality. *European Political Science, 11*(1), 109–124.
Amorim-Maia, A., Anguelovski, I., Chu, E., & Connolly, J. (2022). Intersectional climate justice: A conceptual pathway for bridging adaptation planning, transformative action, and social equity. *Urban Climate, 41*. https://doi.org/10.1016/j.uclim.2021.101053
Axon, S. (2019). Warning: Extinction ahead! Theorizing the spatial disruption and place contestation of climate justice activism. *Environment, Space, Place, 11*(2), 1–26. https://doi.org/10.5749/envispacplac.11.2.0001
BBC. (2018). *Extinction Rebellion: The story behind the activist group*. BBC News Accessed on 11 March 2024 from https://www.bbc.com/news/av/science-environment-46626582
Bennet, W., & Livingston, S. (2018). The disinformation order: Disruptive communication and the decline of democratic institutions. *European Journal of Communication, 33*(2), 122–139.

Brown, G., El-Erian, M., Spence, M., & Lidow, R. (2023). *Permacrisis: A plan to fix a fractured world*. Simon & Schuster.

Burke, S., Sanson, A., & Van Hoorn, J. (2018). The psychological effects of climate change on children. *Current Psychiatry Reports, 20*, 35. https://doi.org/10.1007/s11920-018-0896-9

Bush, G. (2001). *Statement by the President in his address to the nation*. Accessed on 18 March 2024 from https://georgewbush-whitehouse.archives.gov/news/releases/2001/09/20010911-16.html

Castells, M. (1999). *Information technology, globalization and social development* (Discussion Paper No. 114). Geneva: United Nations Research Institute for Social Development Retrieved on 21 October 2024 from https://cdn.unrisd.org/assets/library/papers/pdf-files/dp114.pdf

Christensen, C., Raynor, M., & McDonald, R. (2015). Disruptive innovation. *Harvard Business Review, 93*(12), 44–53.

Chow, J. K. F., & Kennedy, K. (2014). Secondary analysis of large-scale assessment data: An alternative to variable-centred analysis. *Educational Research and Evaluation, 20*(6), 469–493.

Claudia, M. (2022). Psychological effects of fake news—Literature review. *Journal of Educational Sciences & Psychology, 12*(2), 95–103.

Clayton, S. (2020). Climate anxiety: Psychological responses to climate change. *Journal of Society Disorders, 74*, 102263. https://doi.org/10.1016/j.janxdis.2020.102263

Collins, P., & Chepp, V. (2013). Intersectionality. In G. Waylen, K. Celis, J. Kantola, & S. Weldon (Eds.), *Oxford handbook of gender and politics* (pp. 57–87). Oxford University Press.

Cox, M. (2018). *Understanding the global rise of populism*. Accessed on 24 March 2024 from https://www.lse.ac.uk/ideas/Assets/Documents/updates/LSE-IDEAS-Understanding-Global-Rise-of-Populism.pdf

Crenshaw, K. (1989). Demarginalizing the intersection of race and sex: A black feminist critique of antidiscrimination doctrine, feminist theory and antiracial politics. *University of Chicago Legal Forum, 1*, 139–167.

Crowly, T. (2000). Causes of climate change over the past 1000 years. *Science, 289*(5477), 270–277. https://doi.org/10.1126/science.289.5477.270

Fukuyama, F. (1989). The end of history? *The National Interest, 16*, 3–18.

Gans, J. (2016). *The disruption dilemma*. The MIT Press.

Gidron, N., & Hall, P. (2017). The politics of social status: Economic and cultural roots of the populist right. *The British Journal of Sociology, 68*, S57–S84. https://doi.org/10.1111/1468-4446.12319

Goldmatcher, S. (2024, January 15) Voters look past legal problems to give Trump a big victory. *The New York Times*. Accessed on 19 January 2024 from https://www.nytimes.com/2024/01/15/us/politics/trump-wins-iowa.html

Gradstein, M. (2024). Social status, inequality and populism. *Journal of Comparative Economics* [Online First]. https://doi.org/10.1016/j.jce.2024.02.001

Greenes, T. (2003). Globalization and creative destruction. *Cato Journal, 22*(3), 543–558.

Grzanka, P. (2020). From buzzword to critical psychology: An invitation to take intersectionality seriously. *Women & Therapy*, [First Online] https://doi.org/10.1080/02703149.2020.1729473

Han, H., & Ahn, S. (2020). Youth mobilization to stop global climate change: Narratives and impact. *Sustainability, 12*, 4127. https://doi.org/10.3390/su12104127

Huntington, S. (2011). *The clash of civilizations and the remaking of world order*. Simon & Schuster.

Huttunen, K., Møen, J. & Salvanes, K. (2006). *How destructive is creative destruction? The costs of worker displacement* (IZA Discussion Papers, No. 2316), Institute for the Study of Labor (IZA), Bonn Accessed on 28 January 2024 from http://hdl.handle.net/10419/34092

Islam, N., & Winkel, J. (2017). *Climate change and social inequality Department of Economic & Social Affairs (DESA)* (Working Paper No. 152) ST/ESA/2017/DWP/152. Accessed on 12 March 2024 from https://www.un.org/esa/desa/papers/2017/wp152_2017.pdf.

James, P. (2019). The social imaginary in theory and practice. In C. Hudson & E. Wilson (Eds.), *Revisiting the global imaginary* (pp. 33–47). Palgrave Macmillan.

References

Kaplinsky, R. (2011). Schumacher meets Schumpeter: Appropriate technology below the radar. *Research Policy, 40*(2), 193–203.

Kaisara, G., Mare, A., & Peel, C. (2021). Haven't we been here before? A critical analysis of the Fourth Industrial Revolution. In 2021 Conference on Information Communications Technology and Society, Durban, April, 67–72. Retrieved on 21 October 2024 from https://doi.org/10.1109/ICTAS50802.2021.9395028

Kennedy, K. (2023). The Fourth Industrial Revolution: Humanoids, humanity and agency. In K. Kennedy, M. Pavlova, & J. C. K. Lee (Eds). *Soft skills and hard values meeting education's 21st century challenges* (pp. 37–49). Routledge.

Kennedy, K., & Henderson, D. (2024). *Curriculum, pedagogy and assessment*. Pearson Australia.

Kim, K. (2022). *Economic analysis: Russia-Ukraine war impact on supply chains and inflation*. Retrieved on 21 October from https://kpmg.com/kpmg-us/content/dam/kpmg/pdf/2022/economic-analysis-russia-ukraine-war-impact-supply-chains-inflation.pdf

Klinenberg, E., Araos, M., & Kozlov, L. (2020). Sociology and the climate emergency. *Annual Review of Sociology, 46*, 557–577.

Komlos, J. (2014). *Has creative destruction become more destructive?* (Working Paper 20379), National Bureau of Economic Research (NBER). Accessed on 28 January 2024 from http://www.nber.org/papers/w20379

Kop, M. (2022). Abundance and equality. *Frontiers in Research Metrics and Analytics, 7*. https://doi.org/10.3389/frma.2022.977684

Langlois, R. (2002). *Schumpeter and the obsolescence of the entrepreneur* (Economics Working Papers. 200219), Department of Economics, University of Connecticut. Accessed on 24 January 2024 from https://opencommons.uconn.edu/econ_wpapers/200219

Moll, I. (2022). *Debunking the myth of the Fourth Industrial Revolution* (Occasional Paper), University of the Witwatersrand, Access on 7 February 2024 from https://www.wits.ac.za/media/wits-university/faculties-and-schools/humanities/research-entities/real/documents/debunking-the-myth-of-4IR.pdf

Myers, S., & Bernstein, A. (2011). The coming health crisis: Indirect health effects of global climate change. *F1000 Biology Reports, 3*(3), https://www.ncbi.nlm.nih.gov/pmc/articles/PMC3042309/

Nela, N., & Parruca, E. (2023). News overexposure on the actual capacities and the psychological wellbeing during the COVID-19 pandemic: A systemic literature review. *The Global Psychotherapist, 3*(1), 126–132.

Nizami, N. (2019). Industry 4.0 and its creative destruction effects on work in information technology and analytics industry—An empirical analysis. Paper prepared for the 6th Conference of the Regulating for Decent Work Network, International Labour Office Geneva, Switzerland 8–10 July.

O'Brien, K., Selboe, E., & Hayward, B. M. (2018). Exploring youth activism on climate change: dutiful, disruptive, and dangerous dissent. *Ecology and Society, 23*(3). https://doi.org/10.5751/ES-10287-230342

Peters, M. (2017). Technological unemployment: Educating for the Fourth Industrial Revolution. *Educational Philosophy and Theory, 49*(1), 1–6.

Reuters. (2024, January 19). What does Red Sea disruption mean for Europe's economy? *The Standard*. Accessed on 19 January 2024 from https://www.thestandard.com.hk/breaking-news/section/6/212595/What-does-Red-Sea-disruption-mean-for-Europe's-economy

Rizvi, F. (1993). Broadbanding equity in Australian schools. Keynote Address, Biennial Conference of the Australian Curriculum Studies Association, Brisbane. In I. Macpherson (Ed.). *Curriculum in profile: Quality or inequality. Conference report: Curriculum 93*. Canberra: Australian Curriculum Studies Association.

Robinson, K. (2023). What is Hamas? *Council on Foreign Affairs*. Accessed on 19 March 2024 from https://www.cfr.org/backgrounder/what-hamas

Rosenberg, N. (2000). *Schumpeter and the endogeneity of technology: Some American perspectives*. Routledge

Rotenstreich, N. (1971). The idea of historical progress and its assumptions. *History and Theory, 10*(2), 197–221.

Said, E. (1993). *Culture and imperialism*. Vintage.

Savell, S. (2023). *How death outlives war—The reverberating impact of the post 9/11 was on human health*. Watson Institute for International and Public Affairs. Accessed on 19 March 2024 from https://watson.brown.edu/costsofwar/files/cow/imce/papers/2023/Indirect%20Deaths.pdf

Schumpeter, J. (1934). *The theory of economic development* (R. Opie, Trans.). Harvard University Press.

Schumpeter, J. (1942). *Capitalism, socialism, and democracy.*

Schiølin, K. (2020). Revolutionary dreams: Future essentialism and the sociotechnical imaginary of the fourth industrial revolution in Denmark. *Social Studies of Science, 50*(4), 542–566.

Schwab, K. (2016). *The Fourth Industrial Revolution*. World Education Forum.

Simon, Z., & Tamm, M. (2021). Historical futures. *History and Theory, 60*(1), 3–22. https://doi.org/10.1111/hith.12190

Skog, D., Wimelius, H., & Sandberg, J. (2018). Digital disruption. *Business and Information Systems Engineering, 60*(5), 431–437.

Sobel, R., & Clements, J. (2020). *The essential Joseph Schumpeter (Essential Scholars)*. Fraser Institute.

Steinfield, L., Venugopal, S., Appau, S., Barrios, A., Dadzie, C., Gau, R., Holt, D., Mai, N. T., & Shultz, C. (2021). Across time, across space, and intersecting in complex ways: A framework for assessing impacts of environmental disruptions on nature-dependent prosumers. *Journal of Public Policy & Marketing, 40*(2), 262–284. https://doi.org/10.1177/0743915620976563

Stern, D., & Kaufman, S. (2014). Anthropogenic and natural causes of climate change. *Climatic Change, 122*, 257–269. https://doi.org/10.1007/s10584-013-1007-x

Stiglitz, J. (2016). Joseph Stiglitz says standard economics is wrong. Inequality and unearned income kill the economy. Accessed on 8 February 2024 from https://evonomics.com/joseph-stiglitz-inequality-unearned-income/

Suarez-Alvarez, J. (2021). *Are 15-year-olds prepared to deal with fake news and misinformation?* (PISA in Focus, No. 113), OECD Publishing. https://doi.org/10.1787/6ad5395e-en.

Taylor, C. (2004). *Modern social imaginaries*. Duke University Press.

Technorealism. (2021). *Technorealism*. Accessed on 9 February 2024 from https://www.technorealism.org/

Tharoor, S. (2001, September 26). An optimistic outlook for the 21st century. *The New York Times*. Accessed on 13 March 2024 from https://www.nytimes.com/2001/09/26/opinion/IHT-an-optimistic-outlook-for-the-21st-century.html

Thomas, K., Hardy, R., Lazrus, H., Mendez, M., & Orlove, B. (2019). Explaining differential vulnerability to climate change: A social science review. *Wiley Interdisciplinary Review of Climate Change., 10*(2), 1–18.

Tranter, B., & Booth, K. (2015). Scepticism in a changing climate: A cross-national study. *Global Environmental Change, 33*, 154–164.

van Kesteren, F., Altaf, A., & de Weerd, R. (2019). *Trickle up: How pro-poor investments drive economic development synthesis study*. Accessed on 8 February from https://www.partos.nl/wp-content/uploads/2021/05/Trickle-up-How-pro-poor-investments-drive-economic-development.pdf

Venturini, F. (2022). Intelligent technologies and productivity spillovers: Evidence from the Fourth Industrial Revolution. *Journal of Economic Behavior and Organization, 194*, 220–243.

Woodward, A. (2019). Climate change: Disruption, risk and opportunity. *Global Transitions, 1*, 44–49. https://doi.org/10.1016/j.glt.2019.02.001

Zappone, C. (2024, March 14). Trump, trolls and Russia's plot to reshape the world. *Sydney Morning Herald*. Accessed on 15 March 2024 from https://www.watoday.com.au/world/north-america/trump-trolls-and-russia-s-plot-to-reshape-the-world-20240229-p5f8t8.html

Open Access This chapter is licensed under the terms of the Creative Commons Attribution-NonCommercial-NoDerivatives 4.0 International License (http://creativecommons.org/licenses/by-nc-nd/4.0/), which permits any noncommercial use, sharing, distribution and reproduction in any medium or format, as long as you give appropriate credit to the original author(s) and the source, provide a link to the Creative Commons license and indicate if you modified the licensed material. You do not have permission under this license to share adapted material derived from this book or parts of it.

The images or other third party material in this book are included in the book's Creative Commons license, unless indicated otherwise in a credit line to the material. If material is not included in the book's Creative Commons license and your intended use is not permitted by statutory regulation or exceeds the permitted use, you will need to obtain permission directly from the copyright holder.

Chapter 2
Preparing Young People for Disruptive Futures: How Can Education Contribute?

Abstract Over time, education has played an important role in preparing young people as future citizens, workers and community members. Leaders have emerged with knowledge of the future and skills to contribute to social, political and economic development. The major assumption underlying this role has been a knowable future. Yet as shown in the previous chapter the future is no longer stable and the same education will no longer serve young people. New and radical ways are needed for the future preparation of young people for a largely unknown future. This chapter seeks to understand education in its historical contexts examining both quality and theoretical issues that construct education in particular ways. Current issues such as large-scale assessments are examined for their potential as future information sources about the preparedness of students for future living. Central to these needed transformations is the school curriculum and its role in focusing on future needs rather than reifying the past. Transitions to new ways of thinking and acting are never easy and this chapter seeks to show how this might be done. Nevertheless, the chapter is the beginning rather than the end of an important conversation.

Keywords Skills · Education future · Contexts · Transformation

2.1 Introduction

Education as a social process has always served multiple and often conflicting purposes. Currently, it is seen as an essential process supporting the development of modern nation states as well as an individual process facilitating personal growth and development. In ancient times, it was reserved for the children of wealthy parents, although in China a meritocratic system developed that attempted to give access to other than the wealthy. With industrial development in the West, the need for a more educated workforce developed. Education was gradually extended, in Western contexts often with the support of religion. This extension was in the form of very basic forms of education. Numeracy and literacy skills were highlighted to support the needs for new industry development as well as religious engagement.

At the same time, however, in countries such as the United Kingdom, the United States and Australia, other forms of education were available for young people whose parents could afford it. Public schools, so well known in the United Kingdom as private fee paying schools, were duplicated in colonial Australia and continue to this day referred to as greater public schools (GPS). Private schools led the way in the United States predating the public school systems so well known in the twentieth century. Colonization on a broad scale led to the duplication of this system in many Asian and African contexts. Diocesan Girls School, for example, is a continual reminder of colonial influence in what is now China's Hong Kong as is the Diocesan School for Girls in the Eastern Cape of South Africa. The development of multiple forms of education has resulted in dual systems of education. This development can be characterized in its original forms as literacy and numeracy for the poor, French and Latin for the rich. Serving multiple purposes and multiple populations, education's capacity for providing common solutions to the problem of modern disruptions is at best problematic.

Given the potential role of education to prepare young people for navigating multiple disruptions, it is important to understand the challenges this presents. These challenges will be discussed throughout this chapter with a consideration of the following:

- historical developments in education in relation to changing aims and purposes.
- quality issues in education and their potential to inform education for disruption.
- theoretical constructions of schooling—how they help in understanding disruptions.
- community pressure on schools: can national and international testing help with disruptions?
- the school curriculum and its changing foci.

2.2 Historical Developments in Education—Changing Aims and Purposes

Education has always been rationed. In ancient times in countries we know today as Greece and China formal education was not considered as important for girls as it was for boys. Gender was not the only basis on which discrimination took place. In Greece, slaves and their children were not entitled to education, and in Rome, poorer girls would often leave school early to help their families and even to get married. In Ancient China, there was little consideration that education was important for girls even in the most well-off families. This was not so for boys for whom the development of values and skills was seen as important. One aspect of Chinese education was the adoption of a meritocratic process that enabled boys from poor families to compete for entrance to the civil service. Education in these contexts was seen as 'value-adding', but only for some. What was more, even in such contexts education was standardized. It often depended on families themselves, private tutors and values reflecting those of the state rather than supporting individual growth and development. What has changed?

This is a difficult question to answer. On the one hand, it is clear that in many countries education has been extended to all students—males and females, rich and poor and multiple races and ethnicities. Despite this generalization, there are exceptions both within and across countries suggesting that the rationing of education is still part of global education provision. In terms of total net primary school attendance rate, for example, most countries registered in the high 90s. The exceptions are many African countries where the rate ranges from 56.5% for Mali to 98.4% for South Africa. The lowest attendance rate was registered by Afghanistan at 47.2% (Our World in Data, 2025). These are dramatic figures showing how education is rationed significantly in Afghanistan that has banned girls from participating at any level. Many other countries maintain their level of secondary enrolments with some decline when it comes to upper secondary (although the United States maintains a 96% enrolment rate at this level). But African countries in particular register significantly lower rates at upper secondary. Thus, education is not distributed equally on a global scale with significant equity issues particularly in Africa. But what about within countries?

The Gender Report as part of the Global Monitoring Report 2020 (Global Monitoring Report Team, 2020) tended to paint a positive picture of 25 years of progress on gender issues in education. But the picture presented also highlighted many in country equity issues related to gender:

- In at least 20 countries, hardly any poor, rural young woman complete upper secondary school.
- In 24 countries participating in PISA 2018, over 70% of poor boys did not achieve the minimum reading proficiency level.
- The most disadvantaged women are further left behind in terms of literacy skills. In 59 countries, women aged 15–49 from the poorest households are 4 times more likely to be illiterate than those from the richest households.
- Women with disabilities tend to be particularly disadvantaged. In Mozambique, 49% of men with disabilities can read and write, compared with 17% of women with disabilities (p. 1).

Thus, some groups and individuals within countries are deprived of education on account of gender, ethnicity, poverty, location, etc. Education is rationed for these people, while others benefit from a much broader and more inclusive approach. Gilborn (2003) made this point with specific reference to school practices:

> This rationing of education can be seen in many ways. Our research revealed, for example, the use of additional classes for certain pupils; the use of 'mentoring' and progress meetings with senior members of staff; and the provision of new resources (such as textbooks) where others (the hopeless cases) might have to make do with photocopied chapters or hand-outs. This form of educational triage also explains why in many schools the most experienced teachers are increasingly to be found in the second or third teaching group (rather than the 'top' group as used to be the case): it is here, with the suitable cases for treatment, that their skills are judged to have the greatest potential pay-off. (p. 7)

There is an old theme in this quote—some get more, others get less. It was so in ancient societies, and despite the extension of compulsory education in most countries, it remains so today at both local and global levels. Ball et al. (2012) reinforced his point based on their study of a sample of schools in the United Kingdom some ten years after the Gilborn (2003) study referred to above. They concluded that there "is a definitive move away from any attempt to create a common or universal or comprehensive form of education and towards (or back to) one which characterises, classifies and specialises students distributed along a scale, around a norm" (p. 532).

While the studies referred to here are in the one country and draw on small samples of schools, there are likely to be similarities elsewhere. Where ever there is streaming of students into different 'tracks', for example academic and vocational, or when parents decide to opt out of public education and select a private school education for their children or when some measure of student ability dictates that some students should study languages and advanced forms of mathematics while others are directed to technology studies (what used to be called 'wood work', 'metal work' 'home economics' and 'technical drawing'), then differentiation rather than commonality marks students educational experiences. Why is differentiation considered to be problematic?

Within communities and among scholars, there will be considerable debate on this issue. But if we want to rely on education to address issues of disruption and change and prepare students to navigate these processes, we must be able to guarantee some form of common education. Disruptions will affect everyone so everyone needs to be prepared for them. This cannot happen in systems of education that insist on providing differentiated forms of education. The issue is particularly important if, as shown by research, it is often the less well-off students or students from ethnic backgrounds or students with special needs or female students whose educational experiences are limited in some ways. There can be no limits for any students if education to help students cope with disruption is to be successful. This will take some fundamental rethinking about educational provisions across all countries especially as it relates to notions of quality in education. This issue will be taken up in the following section.

2.3 Quality Issues in Education and Their Potential to Inform Education for Disruption

Quality in education became a focus for education systems and education scholars in the twentieth century. Yet the meaning of 'quality' is not always clear. It could refer to the curriculum—standards based, outcomes based, discipline based, integrated or interdisciplinary. Alternatively, it could refer to students' assessment results—especially national and international assessment. It may also refer to school leaders and whether they are instructional leaders, transformational leaders, social justice leaders or servant leaders. It could also refer to pedagogies and teaching strategies and whether direct instruction, inquiry learning, collaborative learning, etc., produce the best academic results. The term quality is also used in relation to teachers. High-quality teachers, it is argued, are most impactful on student learning while poor-quality teachers achieve the reverse results.

If education is to be used to help students navigate complex disruption in their lives and in society, we need to understand how best to do this. The United Nations (UN) designated 'Quality Education' as its fourth sustainable development goal (SDG) with a target implementation date of 2030. This is a good starting point for considering conceptions of quality, but as will be shown later it is not the only way to do so. Yet given the global visibility and priority given to the SDGs understanding SDG 4 is of some importance. The goal of SDG 4 is to "ensure inclusive and equitable quality education and promote lifelong learning opportunities for all" (Department of Economic & Social Affairs, 2024). There are five broad target areas that make up the UN's quality education agenda: Access (4.1, 4.2, 4.3 and 4.5), Outcomes (4.4, 4.6 and 4.7), Equity (4.5 and 4b), Facilities (4a) and Teachers (4b). The latter two are more of a facilitative nature supporting the implementation of the more substantive access, outcomes and equity goals. These goals did not eventuate in a vacuum—they were workshopped and discussed extensively (Smith, 2018) but they are not without criticism (Boeren, 2019). To some extent, they represent a move away from access, the traditional focus of much of UNESCO's work in education. The approach adopted to measuring the targets suggests an even greater departure from traditional UNESCO concerns. Yet from the point of view of helping students navigate disruptions, the SDG approach has much to recommend it.

The previous section in this chapter focused on the way education is 'rationed', with some students getting more and other less in terms of resources, curriculum or even teacher welfare. The advantage of the SDG approach, and UNESCO's values in general, is that the focus is on all students. For example (Department of Economic and Social, 2024):

Target 4.1: By 2030, ensure that all girls and boys complete free, equitable and quality primary and secondary education leading to relevant and effective learning outcomes.
Target 4.2: By 2030, ensure that all girls and boys have access to quality early childhood development, care and pre-primary education so that they are ready for primary education.
Target 4.3: By 2030, ensure equal access for all women and men to affordable and quality technical, vocational and tertiary education, including university.

Thus, should SDG4 be fully implemented by 2030 as is planned, it would well serve anti-disruption education that needs to be available for all from the early years through to postsecondary. Despite virtual global endorsement of the UN's SDGs, there is an alternative conceptualization that has almost as much support. The questions are whether the alternative is inclusive as the SDG approach appears to be.

Barrett et al. (2006) distinguished alternative approaches to quality as being "the Progressive/Humanist tradition—quality of classroom processes" (p. 3) and "the World Bank and the economist tradition" (p. 7). The first of these does not correspond exactly to the SDG approach since it goes much further than focusing on classroom processes. Yet it is accurate to say that it fits broadly within a progressivist/humanist tradition that focuses on the flourishing of individuals within a fair and just society. The way the alternative is phrased lacks a basic theoretical formulation focusing instead on the application of a particular way of thinking demonstrated by the work of the World Bank. Yet this approach is important to understand since theory underlying it has been extremely influential.

Barrett et al. (2006) pointed out that "the 'economist' view of education uses quantitative measurable outputs as a measure of quality, for example enrolment ratios and retention rates, rates of return on investment in education in terms of earnings and cognitive achievement as measured in national or international tests" (p. 2). In addition, there is a concern with the effectiveness and efficiency of schooling, especially in relation to costs. Thus, outcomes and costs are related in the sense that schools are expected to achieve efficiencies in producing the highest levels of learning for the least costs: this approach to quality has been adopted by the World Bank and pursued particularly by its economists, yet they did not invent it. To gain some further insight into the origins of an economistic concept of quality, there are several levels of understanding, one practical and the other theoretical.

In a practical sense, the World Bank has always been wedded to a human-capital theoretical view of education. For example, see the work of such World Bank economists as Psacharopoulos (1972) and Patrinos (1997). They focused much of their work on computing the rates of return for investment in education, but their measure of quality was different from that explained by Barrett et al. (2006). As shown in Montenegro and Patrinos (2014), the quality measure used was "years of schooling" (p. 7), a measure accepted by economists for quite some time. This can be regarded as the first measure of quality developed by economists seeking to understand the role education plays in contributing to national economies and to the lives of individuals. Yet it represented only an initial understanding.

Hanushek and Kimko (2000) reviewed different measure of educational quality used by economics researchers such as length of schooling and school enrolment ratios. Yet these are static measures, and "one does not expect that years of schooling will expand in an unbounded manner...in terms of cognitive skills and human-capital quality, however, continual quality growth is more natural, and the underlying growth models are much more readily interpreted" (p. 1185). Thus, they adopted international test scores as measures of school quality, finding direct and positive relationships between such scores and national economic growth across countries. Yet this was more than the adoption of a new quality measure.

Hanushek and Kimko (2000) indicated that their use of international test scores as quality measures was "a direct application of models of endogenous growth" (p. 1184). Not well known outside economic circles, the model has significant implications for education (Kennedy, 2005). Its underlying assumption is that economic growth is stimulated by actions or ideas within the economic system and not external to it. In terms of education, this can mean that the development of human capital to produce knowledgeable and skilful students may have a greater effect on economic development than providing additional resources per student across an education system. In addition, new ideas produced as part of an education process can be taken up by others to produce yet more new ideas—referred to by economists as a 'spillover effect'. Test scores, therefore, represent students' capacity to contribute—the higher the score the greater the capacity. The idea remains contested, but the rationale is more than a simple preference for numbers: it represents a preference for quality.

Labelling an approach as 'economistic' as opposed to 'progressive', therefore, should not necessarily be seen as negative. It may be limited in the sense that it is narrowly economic rather than more inclusive. Yet it highlights an important point concerning student learning that is central to the issues being discussed in this section. In the progressive tradition, plans for student learning, how they learn, how they are assessed and how they are cared for are important. Yet in the end it is how plans influence learning that is important: students require knowledge, skills and values to equip them for the future. Students need to understand disruptions and they need to know how to deal with them. Education that focuses on these outcomes will be best for future students and for society.

2.4 Theoretical Constructions of Schooling—How They Help in Understanding Disruptions

Educators often prefer to focus on practice rather than theory—what to do, when and how. It makes sense in a way since teaching and classrooms are about daily practice. Yet John Dewey (1904) made the point that:

> The teacher who leaves the professional school with power in managing a class of children may appear to superior advantage the first day, the first week, the first month, or even the first year, as compared with some other teacher who has a much more vital command of the psychology, logic, and ethics of development…he (sic) may continue to improve in the mechanics of school management, but he cannot grow as a teacher, an inspirer and director of soul-life. (p. 15)

He concluded that "the thing needful is improvement of education, not simply by turning out teachers who can do better things that are now necessary to do, but rather by changing the conception of what constitutes education" (p. 30).

Dewey's own work was informed by multiple theories—pragmatism, practical reasoning, experience and experiential learning, inquiry, support for democracy, etc., and this always enabled him to explain and expand his thinking. This is an important role for theory—providing a lens on areas of action and seeking to understand them through reflection and theoretical speculation. In this sense, theory and practice are interactive—one fuels the other. That is how theory will be used in this section— as a means of understanding educational practice and the contexts in which it is embedded. This concept of theory will help to understand the broader contexts in which discussions about disruptions take place.

Kennedy and Henderson (2024) showed one way to draw links between theory and practice, with reference to the school curriculum. This is shown in Table 2.1.

This figure shows how theory and practice interact. Its focus is on a single educational phenomenon, the school curriculum. Its main point is to demonstrate the

Table 2.1 Orientations to the school curriculum

Curriculum orientations	Curriculum functions
	Knowledge, skills and values that:
Cultural	Ensure the foundations of society are transmitted to the next generation
Personal	Provide for the intrinsic needs of individuals and groups
Vocational	Ensure that students are equipped with the necessary knowledge and skills enabling them to participate actively in the world of work
Social	Enable society to function in a harmonious way for the benefit of all
Economic	Ensure that the productive capacity of individuals and the nation as a whole is taken into consideration

Source Based on Kennedy and Henderson (2024, p. 33)

multiple ways in which the curriculum can be constructed based on distinctive orientations. The orientations shown in column 1 are the different theoretical perspectives that lead to different practical approaches for the curriculum. It would be possible to identify the curriculum theorists who have supported these orientations. In addition, community stakeholders not only support different orientations but often argue over them as well. Teachers engaged in adapting the curriculum to meet the requirements of the different orientations may not always be aware of the theoretical underpinnings of their work since they focus on the practical—what is to be done in the classroom. Yet, following Dewey, understanding the theoretical constructions of practice can deepen professional knowledge and skills. It is not a case of either theory or practice but how they influence each other. In what follows, a range of theoretical conceptions of education will be reviewed for the purpose of both understanding them and how that can help in preparing young people for confronting and understanding disruptions.

2.4.1 Conflicting Conceptions of Education—How They Help, or Hinder, in Understanding Disruptions

The plural term, 'conceptions', is deliberately used in this heading to signal that there are multiple conceptions that change over time depending on currently popular ideas, experts promoting those ideas and at times their popularity with the public. This process can provide considerable instability as conceptions and theories change. There is no anchor for theoretical conceptions of education—no single dominant way of regarding the different forms it takes in different contexts. Individuals may adhere to one view or another and groups may come together around a single idea. At the same time, groups with different ideas may emerge equally sure that their view is correct. It is important to recognize this ebb and flow of theory and the importance of its transient nature. Some concrete examples will demonstrate this point.

2.4.2 Power—A Central Concept in Education and Social Contexts

As pointed out in the first section of this chapter, the rationing of education has been a constant theme in educational provision, irrespective of cultural or political contexts. The idea is that education is good for some but not others, that some kind of education is good for some while other kinds of education are good for others, that some kinds of schools are good for some while other kinds of schools are good for others. Who decided who gets what and goes where? Foucault would argue that such decisions are made by people in power since, from his perspective, "power is redefined as a texture of human life and relationships" but more graphically:

> …. power can do many things: "It 'excludes', it 'represses', it 'censors', it 'abstracts', it 'makes', it 'conceals'. In fact, power produces; it produces reality; it produces domains of objects and ritual of truth. (Sajadieh, 2016, pp. 2–3)

If we want to educate young people about disruptions using education systems and their schools, power is a central concept. Climate change, food security, war, energy types and supply, green skills, waste management, single use plastics, Sustainable Development Goals—these are all topics that might be included in the school curriculum. Who will decide this? People whose job it is to make curriculum policy decisions. This can include legislators, policymakers, government agencies, curriculum teams and eventually teachers. These are the people with power, and some have more than others as the following case shows.

Associated Press (2019) reported that:

> A Connecticut lawmaker wants to strike climate change from state science standards. A Virginia legislator worries teachers are indoctrinating students with their personal views on global warming. And an Oklahoma state senator wants teachers to be able to introduce alternative viewpoints without fear of losing their jobs.

The context of the above is the United States and the extract indicates that legislators across different states have concerns about climate change education including moving it from the school curriculum. What is more, they have the power to do what they want to see happen. If successful, teachers would not get the chance to make any decisions about climate change education because it would not be an option in the curriculum. What is also shown is that the scientific consensus about the impact of climate change is not reflected in a social consensus about the topic. This is where power—who has it and who does not—plays such an important role. Opponents will struggle over whatever issue is at hand and the winner will be those who have the most power.

The case above is peculiar to the United States. Lakhani et al. (2023), however, reported that "some political leaders and law enforcement agencies around the world are…launching a fierce crackdown on people trying to peacefully raise the alarm". They referred to the "systematic criminalization of environmental defenders…at its core it's about maintaining the power structures in place". Niranjan (2023, October 12) pointed out that "Germany has increasingly cracked down on climate protests as they have grown more disruptive, with police using laws designed to fight organized crime to tap phones, raid homes freeze bank accounts and place activists in preventive detention". "People power" can at times seem to be the only option available to protestors seeking major social change. Yet the power of the state is immense, as shown above, and when brought to bear on civil society it can be overwhelming. Many may see climate change education and climate change policies as essential for the planet, but the power structures in society always need to be considered because those who have the power are, more often than not, in the winning seat. This is an important point to remember when advocating for social change that threatens the status quo and the interests that benefit from it. Students need to understand this very hard reality.

2.4.3 Utilitarianism—Education for What or Whose Purpose?

Seeking to use the curriculum to include content about different kinds of disruptions highlights the social purposes of schooling. It is not a new idea. John Dewey (1923) pointed out that "I take it for granted that we all admit that, so far as the common school system is concerned, the main business must be to prepare the boys and girls and young men and women who come to these schools to be good citizens, in the broadest sense". Another way to understand this use of the curriculum is to see it as one aspect of a major theoretical idea in the history of education—utilitarianism. Jeremy Bentham, as one of the key proponents of utilitarianism, advocated just two principles for developing a school curriculum (Fernex & Mezeix, 2012):

> On the occasion of propounding any extensive plan of useful instruction – in this, as in every other walk of useful art and science, the lover of mankind will propose to himself two main objects: the one to maximise the quantity of use capable of being derived from it, the other to maximise the facility, and hence the promptitude with which each give portion or degree of it may be rendered obtainable. (p. 5)

The emphasis here is on "quantity of use", or what might today be called "useful knowledge". In constructing the curriculum Bentham distinguished between "useful and not merely ornamental instruction" (Itzkin, 1978, p. 307). Latin, Greek, Religious Studies, Music, Logic did not make it into Bentham's curriculum. Subjects such as these, as well as others, reflected very much the existing classical curriculum still operated in many grammar schools in Bentham's days. Bentham's views on education were not entirely novel, as suggested by Tompson (1971). He reported that changes can be identified in a number of grammar schools, although there was often a reluctance to give up Greek and Latin. This trend towards utilitarianism has continued, as reflected in the above quote from John Dewey, and can be seen in the aims of many education systems world-wide. Yet it is not an uncontested trend, as can still be seen in modern discourses on education.

Kak (2019) pointed out that:

there is a rising voice in the West for reemphasizing a classics-based curriculum that includes the earliest texts of the Western tradition. Educators in India have also begun to speak of a similar classics-based curriculum for India…An Indian-culture centered classics curriculum should be dedicated to universal values and principles and in addition to material on literature, philosophy, polity (arthaśāstra as well as earlier texts that speak of checks and balance between the minister and the king), the arts, and history.

Wang (2023) analysed a rising trend in China where parents chose schools for their children where they would be exposed to the Confucian classics and its moral and social precepts. This was amidst China's relentless pursuit of modernization and economic growth that for the parents in his sample needed to be supplemented with older and perhaps more easily understandable values.

This trend across societies to return to the past was labelled by Ball (1993) as 'cultural restorationism', a comment he made with specific reference to conservative governments in the United Kingdom. Their main "policy preoccupation (is) with the re-valorization of traditional forms of education" (p. 195). Seeking refuge in the past is a way of not dealing with the present. This can create problems when attempts are made to include current priorities, such as knowledge and skills needed to cope with disruptions. Conservatives will always resist change, even when it is clearly needed as in the cases of multiple disruptions on society. This resistance can be another barrier to supporting young people to be better equipped for the future.

2.4.4 Neoliberalism—Let the Market Decide

Conservatives look to the past to ensure stability in the present and into the future. For liberals, however, the central issue is freedom (Krause, 2020):

> As a machine of choice, the truly free human is the human with as much choice as possible. Being bound to community restricts choice. Being bound to religion restricts choice. Being bound to nation restricts choice. Borders restrict choice (and also movement). Poverty restricts choice. Servitude (serfdom, slavery, etc.) restrict choice. And yes, as we see today – human biology restricts choice because I didn't get to choose my gender! Culture may also restrict choice. Why do my parents restrict choices for me too? Therefore it is necessary to overcome all of these barriers that restrict one's choice and free movement.

This quest for freedom is historic in nature and was located entirely in a European context. Thinkers and intellectuals such as Denis Diderot, Adam Smith, René Descartes, Jean-Jacques Rousseau and David Hume, and many more, contributed to the development of a line of thinking that was built on the rationalism of the preceding scientific revolution. The basic theme was freedom of the individual—a theme still heard often today. By mid-nineteenth century, this idea had become so powerful that Pope Pius IX issued an encyclical that contained a "syllabus of errors" that condemned a broad range of 'modern' errors including liberalism, rationalism, socialism, communism and more (Pius 1X). But ideas do not die easily and this one lived on. But it also changed as Krause (2020) explained:

Since humans are atomized self-choosing, self-making, and free moving people, rather than the state being the guarantor and liberator of human freedom, the "market" is seen as the best guarantor and liberator of human freedom. Concerning free movement, the free movement of capital (global capitalism, free trade, and the allocation of capital to new places) fits perfectly with the idea of free movement. Concerning choice, the expansion of choices via economic industrialization, trade with other countries and peoples, and so forth, is seen as the perfect realization of the free-choosing individual.

This view takes individualism much further than the classical view of liberalism outlined previously. It is largely a twenty-first-century view and its complexities have been discussed at length by Peters (2023). He argued that neoliberalism is:

> essentially… a short-hand description for free market policies that were developed and implemented in the period when Thatcher and Ronald Reagan came to power in 1979 and 1980 respectively. Essentially, it became known as a set of related public policies that was aimed at deregulating capital markets, embracing 'free trade' globalization, and privatization policies responsible for state assets sale, and the commercialization and corporatization of government departments with the overall aim of paring back the state and increasing individual responsibility. (p. 1574)

He goes on to explain the broader historical context in which these ideas developed and their eventual incorporation into international policy organizations such as the International Monetary Fund, the World Bank and the Organization for Economic Development. The essential element of neoliberalism was the individual freedom of the classical liberals taken to its most extreme limits: not only should individuals be free, but in a neoliberal world institutions should be free as well and allowed to operate without barriers. Peters (2023) drew on Foucault with his final summary that "neoliberalism leads to the birth of biopolitics and the expansion of market logic and competition into all aspects of social life, indeed, as the new set of techniques and mechanisms that reconstituted the social in terms of market values" (p. 1580).

There are several key points to make concerning the above description. Many classical liberals, while espousing individual freedom, argued that the state could play a role in guaranteeing this freedom. There are many progressive liberals today who continue to hold this view especially as shown in the development of regulatory frameworks in relation to diversity, equity and inclusion. Yet neoliberals rejected the state entirely shown by the constant calls for 'small government' and the replacement of all state regulation with private enterprises and companies. Nowhere has this been truer than in the realm of education that developed and grew across multiple societies under the direction of governments. Neoliberals introduced the idea of 'school choice' arguing that the state was an inefficient provider. Education, it was argued, would be much better if provision were privately made and parents were free to choose the type of education they wanted for their children.

Viteritti et al. (2005) pointed out that:

> The choice idea is commonly traced to a fifty-year-old essay by the Nobel laureate Milton Friedman, who advocated a market approach to education. Friedman wanted to give all parents a voucher so that they could choose their children's schools from an assortment of public, private, and religious institutions. He believed that the ensuing competition would force the closure of low-performing institutions, and the appropriation of public funding for non public schools would create a market of new educational providers. (p. 138)

This represents the most extreme form of school choice and in this 'pure' deregulated form it has rarely been implemented. Yet there are versions of choice-based policies with charter schools in the United States, academies in the England, vouchers in Sweden, the English Schools Foundation in Hong Kong and international schools in China. Each provides a different way of implementing choice in an education system. In Australia, over a third of students attend independent schools, but these differ from the previous examples. These are largely religious schools, examples of which can also be found in England, the United States and Hong Kong. While they provide 'choice', it is largely a choice between religious (i.e., conservative) and public values. Neoliberal choice, however, is more likely to focus on choosing between schools with high academic standards and those with low standards. This could be between schools within a single school system or even within school districts (for example, in the United States) or between systemic state schools and newly established charter schools. In all cases, it is parents who make the choice, for whatever reason, but largely because they want the best educational experience and outcomes for their children.

Yet choice theory and policy create problems for education about disruptions. Hong Kong's Direct Subsidy Schools (DSS) provide a good example. They are subsidized financially by the government, are expected to provide additional resources through school fees and are not required to follow the local curriculum. This latter flexibility is similar to most non-state schools, whether established for conservative reasons or to achieve higher standards for student learning. In this context, what responsibility will deregulated schools and school systems have for preparing young people to both understand and cope with future disruptions? In the future, this will be a major problems for choice theorists: disruptions will not differentiate types of schools or their graduates, all of whom will be subject to disruptive destruction.

2.4.5 Poststructuralism—Or No Theory?

Gannon (2006) pointed out that "poststructuralism upsets humanism's basic tenets: subjects who are coherent and stable, language that is transparent, knowledge as truth produced through reason" (p. 491). Gibson-Graham (2000) adds "while knowledge is understood within a modernist frame as singular, cumulative and neutral, from a poststructuralist perspective knowledge is multiple, contradictory, and powerful" (p. 95). Poststructuralism, therefore, has challenged the Enlightenment tradition of rationalism, the scientific tradition of empiricism and knowledge building and the idea of freedom as an essentialist construct meant to apply to society in general. There are no essentialist constructs in poststructuralism, just individuals, on their own, seeking their own truth in an unknown world unlikely to yield it. Gannon (2006) described the contingent nature of poststructuralist knowledge when she referred to some who have been recognized as leaders of this theoretical tradition:

These authors write themselves as unreliable and contradictory narrators who speak the self— the multiple selves that each of them is and have been—in discontinuous fragments informed by memory, the body, photographs, other texts, and, most importantly, other people. (p. 491)

There is no certainty in a poststructuralist world—it is a contingent world that can only be navigated by intuition guided by 'knowledge' that is always suspect. It is not uncommon for poststructuralism itself to be called "disruptive' when it constantly challenges accepted wisdom, especially related to Western thought and ideas. It is unlikely to see the kind of disruptions portrayed in this book as anything more than part of a broad imaginary constructed by elites. While there are some encouraging signs of engagement on issues such as climate change (Dujardin, 2019), for the most part poststructuralists maintain an "incredulity towards metanarratives" (Lyotard, 1984). They prefer instead to interrogate local conditions rather than conditions that are said to apply to all in a hegemonic manner. Using poststructuralism as a theoretical frame, therefore, is unlikely to be an effective tool to confront the challenges that have so far been discussed in this book.

The final point to make in this section is that different theories have implications for both understanding disruptions and engaging with strategies designed to overcome them. Theories act as lenses through which disruptions can be interrogated. But care is needed to understand the potential of different theories for confronting disruptions rather than retreating from necessary action for survival.

2.5 Community Pressure on Schools: Can National and International Testing Help with Disruptions?

International large-scale assessments such as the Organization for Economic Development's (OECD) Program for International Student Assessment (PISA) and the International Association for the Evaluation of Educational Achievement's (IEA) Trends in International Mathematics and Science Study (TIMSS), Progress In International Reading Literacy Study (PIRLS) and the International Civic and Citizenship Education Study (ICCS) are very much part of the global education landscape. Add to these the National Assessment of Educational Progress (NAEP) in the United States, the National Assessment Program (NAP) in Australia, National Curriculum Tests in England, Annual National Assessments (ANA) in South Africa and we can see how education policymakers, as well as test designers and measurement experts, have opted for standardized testing as a means of determining not only student achievement but the quality of education as well. The question is how important are these in confronting the challenges and disruptions characterizing current times?

Despite the consensus on the importance of testing programmes by policymakers and test designers, such consensus has not always extended to the academic community (Bank, 2012; Berliner, 2011; Grey & Morris, 2024; Zhao, 2020; Hopmann, 2008). Not all views from the academy have been negative. Carnoy and Rothstein

2.5 Community Pressure on Schools: Can National and International ... 41

(2013), for example, argued that international assessments provided a better understanding of the achievement for disadvantaged students in the United States while De Bortoli and Thomson (2009) argued that the disadvantage suffered by Australia's indigenous students was better understood based on a review of PISA results. In any event, the advice of Rutkowski and Rutkowski (2016), both supporters of large-scale assessments, is well made. They argued that PISA data needs to be interpreted carefully, limitations need to be clearly acknowledged and technical information should be made available as soon as possible after the release of results. Policymakers are often too quick to respond and secondary data analysis not based on a clear understanding of the data's limitations can be misleading. Against this background we can make a more accurate assessment of the usefulness of such data for the future.

There are some key issues to consider:

- The advantages and limitations of large sample research.
- The nature of content in large-scale assessments—knowledge, skills and attitudes.
- Question style—multiple choice versus open-ended questions.
- Relationship of assessment to curriculum.

2.5.1 Advantages and Limitations of Large Sample Research

There is little doubt that having access to large samples of participants provides the opportunity to ask challenging questions that can be interpreted with diverse samples and multiple contexts. PISA 2022, for example, surveyed around 6,900,000 15-year-olds in 81 countries focusing on mathematics knowledge and skills as well as reading and science. Having access to so many diverse students and contexts has the benefit of collecting rich data that can help to understand current levels of knowledge and skills on virtually unlimited topics. Of course, PISA is limited to three broad areas of inquiry, but the possibility of expanding into areas of greater relevance to disruptions is clearly something that could be explored.

Endorsing the potential of large sample research is not to dismiss other kinds of research involving small samples. Interview and observational studies using limited samples have a key role to play in understanding phenomena whose meaning is unclear. Questions can be used to probe responses, and lengthy observations can provide a perspective over time. Deep theoretical issues can also be explored with small samples. The issue about which research method to use is not an ideological question and it should not be an issue of what skills a researcher possesses. Rather, it is a matter of what research questions we wish to answer—choose the question, then the best research methods that can help to address it. There may well be key issues related to disruptions that small sample research could help to answer, but it is not our purpose to explore those here.

Despite the usefulness of large sample research, there are also limitations. For example, in a publication authored by the Director of OECD's Directorate of Education, the following statement appeared: "the PISA assessment in 2022, represent(ed) about 29 million 15-year-olds" (Schleicher, 2023). The assumption being made here is that the sample of 690,000 students represented the total population of 15-year-olds in the 81 countries participating in PISA 2022. Rutkowski and Rutkowski (2016), however, showed that this level of generalizability in PISA data is highly questionable and that there are certainly variations across countries that indicate the PISA sample is not representative of the whole population of 15-year-olds. Sampling, therefore, can be a limitation in the interpretation of PISA data with generalizability, meaning the application of the results outside the sample,limited. The data needs to be treated for what it is: individual responses from a large group that may, or may not, be indicative of the views of a larger group. It is more than a simple technical issue. It does not invalidate the data, but it does restrict its application.

For the future, we need to take what large sample research to offer and develop ways in which it can be used to support young people in both understanding disruptions and responding to them. The technology of this kind of assessment is well developed to the point where most of it now is online and therefore accessible, at least in those jurisdictions where this is possible. There are also some ways in which such assessment can be made better suited to broader purposes than assessing student achievement in school subjects. These ways will be discussed in the following sections.

2.5.2 The Nature of Content in Large-Scale Assessments—'Knowledge, Skills and Attitudes'

While PISA focuses on discipline knowledge, it is most often in an applied context. It evaluates the extent to which students can apply knowledge to a broad range of problems within the broad areas of mathematics, science and reading. Yet PISA is not only about testing knowledge. It has asked questions on a broad range of non-cognitive area areas such as bullying, well-being, feelings, creative thinking and global competence. Some of these might be described as school environment variables, others as personal characteristics and yet others as broad curriculum objectives. They are included to try and develop a more complete picture of student achievement that is influenced by more than exposure to curriculum content and various kinds of teaching strategies. But importantly they signal that large sample assessments are capable of being more inclusive than relying on knowledge accumulation alone.

Like PISA, ICCS, that focuses on civics and citizenship education, separates the content of its test into cognitive items and survey questions that are grouped into two broad areas: attitudes and engagement described like this (Schulz et al., 2018):

> *Attitudes*: these include beliefs about democracy and citizenship, attitudes toward equal rights for groups in society, perceptions of threats to the world's future, trust in groups and institutions, as well as attitudes toward the country of residence. • *Engagement*: these refer to students' self-confidence in undertaking civic activities, past and current engagement at school or in the community, as well as their expectations of future civic action, including constructs such as preparedness to participate in legal or illegal activities to

express their opinion, anticipated future political participation as adults, and anticipated future participation in citizenship activities at school. (p. 22)

Ironically, the results of ICCS' cognitive test grab the public attention whereas the issues raised by the attitudinal and engagement questions are given less attention. Yet it is these latter that could be more important for exploring issues about students' engagement with disruption issues and attitudes towards them. A distinctive feature of ICCS is the use of questions about future intentions to participate in a broad range of possible activities: illegal protests, volunteering and the formal political system. This kind of feedback in relation to specific disruptive events could be especially useful, particularly given the reach of the study to over twenty countries. Yet there would need to be changes to both the purposes and uses of large sample assessments.

Understanding students' levels of academic achievement is an understandable issue for governments and even parents yet it may not be the most significant issue for the future. Equipping young people to face disruptions of various kinds, understanding their skills and values and being aware of how they plan to face the future are likely to be more important. In this case, the current technology of large sample assessments could be an important part of the future.

2.5.3 Question Style—Multiple Choice Versus Open-Ended Questions

There is perhaps a stereotype of the kind of questions included in tests such as PISA, ICCS and TIMSS. The stereotype is simple multiple choice questions with a limited number of response options. Yet large-scale testing has gone beyond such questions with the types of questions asked and the way they are scored. PISA, for example, makes sample questions available and it is possible to see how questions are phrased, the resources provided to help students understand the questions and the reasoning behind asking the questions. Examples can be found here: https://www.oecd.org/pisa/pisaproducts/pisa-test-questions.htm. ICCS has used open-ended response items where students are asked to respond in writing to a question. Multiple markers are used to score the responses and a high level of consensus is required for grades to be awarded at whatever level is agreed. These questions form only a small part of the overall assessment and they are subject to scoring procedures consistent with a psychometric assessment. Yet they show how far large sample assessments have come from simple multiple choice questions.

The question for the future is what further innovations can take place in item format in order to use large sample assessments for broader purposes than measuring student achievement? Currently open-ended items are only a small proportion of the total number of items so one innovation would be to increase the number of open-ended items. This would allow for a broader range of issues to be included. The technology for scoring the answers seems to be well advanced but different technical reports show that there are many technical details to resolve. This suggests that more needs to be known about open-ended questions such as assessment tools, how to develop and score them and how to incorporate them into normal assessment processes. At the same time, as these questions have been developed within the psychometric tradition, there are rules of procedure that need to be followed even as the numbers of such items might increase. There is a certain stability in that tradition in terms of rules and processes and this will be helpful to ensure widespread acceptance of bother the item type and the answers it produces.

2.5.4 Relationship of Assessment to the School Curriculum

TIMSS is related to the school curriculum and is therefore focused on academic achievement in the tested school subjects. PISA, on the other hand, has been designed to test skills and knowledge needed for daily life and living. It might be argued that there should be no difference between "curriculum knowledge" and the knowledge needed for everyday living. This is a crucial distinction when it comes to the knowledge needed for understanding future disruptions, confronting them and developing strategies to overcome them. In this area, that is the main focus of this book, there should not be a gap between curriculum knowledge and knowledge for everyday living. Yet the history of curriculum shows that the gap has always existed: it is now time to close it to ensure young people can face the future not just with confidence but also relevant knowledge, skills and values. The following section will focus on ways that the school curriculum can be reoriented to ensure that it will focus on knowledge for living.

2.6 The School Curriculum and Its Changing Foci: Soft Skills, Outcomes, Censorship and Civic Education

The 'school' curriculum is often seen to be the property of schools, teachers and their students. The reality, however, is that it has a much broader ownership (Kennedy & Henderson, 2024). Governments, parents, business owners and community members all have a stake in what students learn in schools. For example, very often as governments change so does the curriculum to reflect the new government's values and priorities. This means that the curriculum can be contested between different interest groups seeking to promote their view of what is important for students to learn. Contestation is more likely to happen in democratic societies but the interest of governments in the curriculum is as at least as strong in authoritarian societies as it is in democracies. Yet as we move forward in the age of disruption there needs to be a much greater social and political consensus on what students should know, believe and value.

One area where there appears to be a growing consensus is related to the kind of skills needed for the future that moves the curriculum from an exclusive focus on knowledge to a greater emphasis on skills—and in this case, 'soft' skills. Kennedy et al. (2023) showed that there have been multiple skills agendas focused on the assumed needs of the new century. The Partnership for Twenty-First-Century Skills (P21) (Trilling & Fadel, 2009) perhaps gained the most traction. Yet additional formulations of skills' requirements were also made by the European Commission (2016), with its New Skills Agenda, the World Education Forum (2024) and Mc Kinsey (Dondi et al., 2021) with their foci on the future of work and UNESCO, with its focus on transversal skills that also included the values underlying these (ERI-Net, 2016). The commonality among these different foci was the assumption that changes to work and society in the new century required changes not just in skill sets but to the entire school curriculum. But there were also significant differences.

P21 was developed around the existing school curriculum but added skills like creativity, innovation, critical thinking, problem solving, collaboration and more. These also appear in the other frameworks alongside more work-oriented skills related to leadership, digital fluency, self-awareness and self-management. These appear to be stable, but the WEF changes its list every few years based on regular surveys of employers. The difference in skills requirements across the decade from 2015 to 2025 are shown in Kennedy et al. (2023). Most of the movements across time do not make drastic changes—complex problem solving and critical thinking stay in the top 3 for the decade. Yet the employer surveys show that perceptions change over time in response to what employers see as emerging trends. This raises an important issue about contexts and how they may influence the kind of skills thought to be necessary. Are twenty-first-century skills generic or context bound?

This was not exactly the question asked by Muyambo-Gotto et al. (2023), who investigated twenty-first-century skills from the perspective of students in Zimbabwe. Yet their study addresses the broader question about the relevance of context. Their sample of secondary students ranked the following broad areas as crucial for the twenty-first century.

- <u>Self-Management</u>: Productivity and Accountability, Leadership and Responsibility, Initiative and Self-direction, Social and Cross-cultural Skills.
- <u>Learning Skills and Values</u>: (Civic Literacy, Flexibility and Adaptability, Environmental Literacy, Health Literacy, Global Connectivity, Financial, Economic, Business and Entrepreneurial Literacy Creativity and Innovation and Critical Thinking skills).
- <u>Learning Processes</u>: (Information, Media and Technological skills, twenty-first century standards, twenty-first-century Learning Environments and Collaboration skills).

Self-management, the most highly ranked factor, makes sense in the light of the comment in the AFRO Barometer "that Zimbabwean youth (defined here as aged 18–35) have more education than their elders but are also more likely to be unemployed" (Moyo-Nyede & Mpako, 2023). It seems that the Zimbabwean 16- and 17-year-olds who responded to questions about their priorities for twenty-first-century skills were well aware of their context that would not guarantee their employment. Rather, poor employment prospects require them to be self-reliant—thus the importance of self-management for them. Context influenced this response, and different contexts would likely yield different responses elsewhere. New skills may well be needed for the twenty-first century, but contexts appear to be important for determining what those skills should be.

Nevertheless, the Zimbabwean study was small and its generalizability is limited—even within Zimbabwe. Yet it is indicative that more attention should be paid to contexts when considering the skills and knowledge needed for confronting disruptions both now and in the future. Skills formulations derived from Western contexts characterized by new digital and AI-dominated industries will not necessarily meet the needs of diverse communities threatened by rising oceans, ravaging fires, floods and the disappearance of traditional jobs. While the school curriculum in these contexts may still be structured around the traditional academic curriculum, thought needs to be given to ways in which it can be made more relevant to equipping young people both to understand new disruptions and how to confront them. It may mean more interdisciplinary-based approaches to science, the development of advanced critical thinking and problem-solving skills, the development of collaborative and interpersonal skills, a focus on multicultural and intercultural understanding and the diverse contexts in which these are most needed. To this core, local issues and priorities need to find their way into the curriculum so there is a greater understanding of what lies ahead and what needs to be done. It is a significant challenge for local education authorities but one that must be met for the sake of our future.

There are both facilitators and inhibitors in any change process and their affect in the future needs to be well understood. These influences will be the focus of the next chapter thus extending our understanding of the role of education in a future without boundaries.

References

Associated Press. (2019). *Many Republicans want climate change erased from curriculum*. Retrieved on 4 May 2024 from https://www.courthousenews.com/many-republicans-want-climate-change-erased-from-curriculum/
Ball, S. (1993). Education, majorism and 'the curriculum of the dead.' *Curriculum Studies, 1*(2), 195–214. https://doi.org/10.1080/0965975930010202
Ball, S., Maguire, M., Perryman, J., & Hoskins, K. (2012). Assessment technologies in schools: 'Deliverology' and the 'play of dominations.' *Research Papers in Education, 27*(5), 513–533.
Bank, V. (2012). On OECD policies and the pitfalls in economy-driven education: The case of Germany. *Journal of Curriculum Studies, 44*(2), 193–210.
Barrett, A., Chawla-Duggan, R., Lowe, J., Nikel, J., & Ukpo, E. (2006). *Review of the 'international' literature on the concept of quality in education*. Paper produced by EdQual, A Research Programme Consortium in Implementing Educational Quality in Low Income Countries. Retrieved on 21 April 2024 from https://www.edqual.org/publications/workingpaper/edqualwp3.pdf/at_download/file.pdf

References

Berliner, D. C. (2011). The context for interpreting PISA results in the USA. Negativism, chauvinism, misunderstanding, and the potential to distort the educational systems of nations. In M. Pereira, H.-G. Kotthoff & R. Cowen (Eds.), *PISA under examination: Changing knowledge, changing tests, and changing schools* (pp. 77–96). Sense Publishers.

Boeren, E. (2019). Understanding Sustainable Development Goal (SDG) 4 on "quality education" from micro, meso and macro perspectives. *International Review of Education, 65*, 277–294.

Carnoy, M., & Rothstein, R. (2013). *International tests show achievement gaps in all countries, with big gains for U.S. disadvantaged students*. Economic Policy Institute, Washington, DC. Retrieved from http://www.epi.org/blog/international-testsachievement-gaps-gains-american-students/

De Bortoli, L., & Thomson, S. (2009). *The achievement of Australia's Indigenous students in PISA 2000–2006*. https://research.acer.edu.au/ozpisa/6

Department of Economic and Social Affairs. (2024). *Ensure inclusive and equitable quality education and promote lifelong learning opportunities for all*. Retrieved on 23 October 2024 from https://sdgs.un.org/goals/goal4#targets_and_indicators

Dewey, J. (1904). The relation of theory to practice in education. In C. McMurry (Ed.), *The third yearbook of the national society for the scientific study of education* (pp. 9–31), Public School Publishing Company. Retrieved on 29 April 2024 from https://archive.org/details/r00elationoftheorynatirich

Dewey, J. (1923). Social purposes in education. *General Science Quarterly, 7*(2). Retrieved on 5 May 2024 from https://doi.org/10.1002/sce.3730070201

Dondi, M., Klier, J., Panier, F., & Schubert, J. (2021, June 25). *Defining the skills citizens will need in the future world of work* (p. 3). Retrieved on 12 July 2021 from www.mckinsey.com/industries/public-and-social-sector/our-insights/defining-the-skills-citizens-will-need-in-the-future-world-of-work

Dujardin, S. (2019). Planning *with* climate change? A poststructuralist approach to adaptation to climate change. *Annals of the American Association of Geographers, 110*(4), 1059–1074.

ERI-Net. (2016). *School and teaching practices for twenty-first century challenges: Lessons from the Asia-Pacific region*. UNESCO.

European Commission. (2016). *Competence frameworks: The European approach to teach and learn 21st century skills*. Retrieved on 11 June 2024 from https://ec.europa.eu/jrc/en/news/competence-frameworks-european-approach-teach-and-learn-21st-century-skill

Fernex, A., & Mezeix, M. (2012). *A problematization of the concept of utility: Bentham's chrestomatic project*. Retrieved on 5 May 2024 from https://www.stern.nyu.edu/sites/default/files/assets/documents/con_036933.pdf

Gannon, S. (2006). The (im)possibilities of writing the self-writing: French poststructural theory and autoethnography. *Cultural Studies ↔ Critical Methodologies, 6*(4), 474–495.

Gibson-Graham, J. (2000). Poststructural interventions. In E. Sheppard & T. Barnes (Eds.), *Companion to economic geography* (pp. 95–110). Blackwell.

Gilborn, D. (2003). *'Raising standards' or rationing education? Racism and social justice in policy and practice*. Retrieved on 7 April 2024 from https://discovery.ucl.ac.uk/id/eprint/10001640/1/gillborn2001raising105text.pdf

Global Education Monitoring Report Team. (2020). *Global Monitoring Report 2020—Inclusion in education—All means all*. UNESCO.

Grey, S., & Morris, P. (2024). Capturing the spark: PISA, twenty-first century skills and the reconstruction of creativity. *Globalisation, Societies and Education, 22*(2), 156–171. https://doi.org/10.1080/14767724.2022.2100981

Hanushek, E., & Kimko, D. (2000). Schooling, labor-force quality, and the growth of nations. *American Economic Review, 90*(5), 1184–1208.

Itzkin, E. (1978). Bentham's Chrestomathia: Utilitarian legacy to English education. *Journal of the History of Ideas, 39*(2), 303–316.

Hopmann, S. (2008). No child, no school, no state left behind: Schooling in the age of accountability. *Journal of Curriculum Studies, 40*(4), 417–456.

Kak, S. (2019, June 18). An Indian classics curriculum. *Medium*. Retrieved on 6 May 2024 from https://subhashkak.medium.com/an-indian-classics-curriculum-d484969ae458

Kennedy. K. (2005). *Changing Schools for Changing Times–New Directions for the School Curriculum in Hong Kong*. The Chinese University Press.

Kennedy, K., & Henderson, D. (2024). *Curriculum, pedagogy and assessment*. Pearson Australia.

Kennedy, K., Pavlova, M., & Lee, J. C. K. (2023). *Soft skills and hard values—Meeting education's 21st century challenges*. Routledge.

Krause, P. (2020). *The two sides of liberalism*. Retrieved on 10m May 2024 from https://minervawisdom.com/2020/11/21/the-two-sides-of-liberalism/

Lakhani, N., Gayle, D., & Taylor, M. (2023, October 12). How criminalization is being used to silence climate activists across the world. *The Guardian*. Retrieved on 5 March 2024 from https://www.theguardian.com/environment/2023/oct/12/how-criminalisation-is-being-used-to-silence-climate-activists-across-the-world

Lyotard, J. (1984). *The postmodern condition: A report on knowledge*. University of Minnesota Press.

Niranjan, A. (2023, October 12). Threats to Germany's climate campaigners fuelled by politicians' rhetoric. *The Guardian*. Retrieved on 5 May 2024 from https://www.theguardian.com/environment/2023/oct/12/threats-to-germanys-climate-campaigners-fuelled-by-politicians-rhetoric-says-activist

Montenegro, C., & Patrinos, H. (2014). *Comparable estimates of returns to schooling around the world* (Policy Research Working Paper, 7020). World Bank Group, Education Practice Group. Retrieved on 26 April 2024 from https://documents1.worldbank.org/curated/en/830831468147839247/pdf/WPS7020.pdf

Moyo-Nyede, S., & Mpako, A. (2023, December 7). *Young Zimbabweans see their government as falling short on employment and the economy*. AFRO Barometer retrieved on 11 June 2024 from https://www.afrobarometer.org/publication/ad744-young-zimbabweans-see-their-government-as-falling-short-on-employment-and-the-economy/#:~:text=official%20youth%20unemployment%20rate%20(defined,jobs%20(Moyo%2C%202023).

Muyambo-Goto, O., Naidoo, D., & Kennedy, K. (2023). Students' conceptions of 21st century education in Zimbabwe. *Interchange, 54*, 49–80. https://doi.org/10.1007/s10780-022-09483-3

Our World in Data. (2025). *Net attendance rate of primary school 2023*. Retrieved on 18 April 2025 from https://ourworldindata.org/grapher/primary-school-attendance-selected-countries

Patrinos, H. (1997). Differences in education and earnings across ethnic groups in Guatemala. *The Quarterly Review of Economics and Finance, 37*(4), 809–821.

Peters, M. (2023). The early origins of neoliberalism: Colloque Walter Lippman (1938) and the Mt Perelin Society (1947). *Educational Philosophy and Theory, 55*(14), 1574–1581.

Pius IX. (1864). *The syllabus of errors*. Retrieved on 24 October 2024 from https://www.globalendeavor.net/RevRev_CC/phase%204%20docs/2019-06-25_1864-12-08_v2_Syllabus-of-Errors_Pope-Piux-IX_text.pdf

Psacharopoulos, G. (1972). Rates of return on investment in education around the world. *Comparative Education, 16*(1), 54–67.

Rutkowski, L., & Rutkowski, D. (2016). A call for a more measured approach to reporting and interpreting PISA results. *Educational Researcher, 45*(4), 252–257. https://doi.org/10.3102/0013189X16649961

Sajadieh, N. (2016). Foucault and educational theory. In M. Peters (Ed.), *Encyclopedia of educational philosophy and theory* (pp. 1–5). Springer. https://doi.org/10.1007/978-981-287-532-7_146-1

Schleicher, A. (2023). PISA 2022-Insights and Interpretations. OECD. Retrieved on 18 April 2025 from https://www.hm.ee/sites/default/files/documents/2023-12/PISA%202022%20Insights%20and%20Interpretations_OECD.pdf

Schulz, W., Carstens, R., Losito, B., & Fraillon, J. (2018). *ICCS 2016 Technical Report*. IEA.

References

Smith, W. (2018). One indicator to rule them all: How SDG 4.1.1 dominates the conversation and what it means for the most marginalized. In A. Wiseman (Ed.), *Annual Review of Comparative and International Education, 37*, 27–34. https://doi.org/10.1108/S1479-367920190000037002

Tompson, S. (1971). The English grammar school curriculum in the 18th century: A reappraisal. *British Journal of Educational Studies, 19*(1), 32–39.

Trilling, B., & Fadel, C. (2009). *21st century skills: Learning for life*. Jossey Boss.

Viteritti, J, Walberg, H., & Wolf, P. (2005). School choice: How an abstract idea became a political reality. *Brookings Paper on Education Policy, 8*. Accessed on 12 May 2024 from http://www.jstor.org/stable/20062557

Wang, C. L. (2023). Interweaving nationalism and cosmopolitanism in the cultivation of Confucian citizens through classics reading in contemporary China. *Citizenship Teaching and Learning, 18*(3), 251–368.

World Education Forum. (2024). *Skills for the future: 4 ways to help workers transition to the digital economy*. Retrieved on 24 October 2024 from https://www.weforum.org/agenda/2024/10/jobs-skills-work-digital-economy/

Zhao, Y. (2020). Two decades of havoc: A synthesis of criticism against PISA. *Journal of Educational Change, 21*(2), https://doi.org/10.1007/s10833-019-09367-x

Open Access This chapter is licensed under the terms of the Creative Commons Attribution-NonCommercial-NoDerivatives 4.0 International License (http://creativecommons.org/licenses/by-nc-nd/4.0/), which permits any noncommercial use, sharing, distribution and reproduction in any medium or format, as long as you give appropriate credit to the original author(s) and the source, provide a link to the Creative Commons license and indicate if you modified the licensed material. You do not have permission under this license to share adapted material derived from this book or parts of it.

The images or other third party material in this book are included in the book's Creative Commons license, unless indicated otherwise in a credit line to the material. If material is not included in the book's Creative Commons license and your intended use is not permitted by statutory regulation or exceeds the permitted use, you will need to obtain permission directly from the copyright holder.

Chapter 3
Shaping Education Futures: What Will Hinder and What Will Facilitate Change?

Abstract There is general agreement that education plays an important socializing function for both young and old. Nations invest a considerable proportion of their budgets to ensure that young people are equipped with basic knowledge and skills to equip them with the tools they will need to be productive workers, active citizens and compassionate human beings. Yet in recent times education has been contested in many communities with attempts at censorship of the knowledge students can access, the promotion of nationalism over globalism and ongoing racism that characterizes many societies in which schools are embedded. New digital technologies and artificial intelligence are often seen to offer solutions for the future, but they also create new problems that need to be resolved. At the same time there are also issues such as censorship, nationalism and anti-diversity that are not amenable to technological solutions. All these can act as barriers to a more positive role for education. These issues will be reviewed in this chapter along with peace education in an attempt to identify how education can be constructed positively despite potentially negative barriers.

Keywords Socialization · Nationalism · Globalism · Technology · Diversity censorship

3.1 Introduction

UNESCO has championed the idea of "futures literacy" arguing that anticipating the future can help not only the future but the present as well. Miller (2018) argued that "the imperative is to colonise tomorrow with today's idea of tomorrow" (p. 21). Yet this conflation linking 'today and tomorrow' is problematic. Wynter and McKittrick (2015), for example, argued the need to "give humanity a different future" (pp. 72–73) by which they meant a non-racialized, secular, non-discriminatory and inclusive future. For them this would require the kind of significant epistemological break such as that characterized centuries ago by Copernicus' support for a heliocentric view of the solar system. He challenged the Christian church's assumptions related to the well-accepted Ptolemaic or geocentric view of our planet. His challenge was not a case of seeking compromise with the thought leaders of the day. Copernicus' views represented a paradigm shift that eventually provided the foundations for scientific and social revolutions despite the Christian church's very active opposition. The call for a 'new humanity' in the future requires a similar scale of paradigmatic change: its purpose is to eliminate those parts of today that have been dehumanizing and create a fair and just future for the whole of humanity.

Copernican-like revolutions do not happen every day. Yet there can always be a commitment to leaving behind what has injured, damaged and suppressed some people in order to build up others. In future, we need to be able to draw on all of humanity to confront disruptions. This will involve the multiple intelligences of the whole population in order to draw on the best ideas and strategies available. The challenge is to remove barriers to a complete understanding of what lies ahead and to focus on capacities that will assist in confronting and overcoming future disruptions. In this chapter, both barriers to understanding disruptions and facilitators that can assist that understanding will be reviewed in order to develop a sense of how positive education can help shape the future.

The following issues will be examined to assess their contribution, either positive or negative, for shaping education as a powerful force for the future:

- Censorship and today's 'anti-woke' movement
- Nationalism, patriotism and love for country
- Diversity, racism and discrimination
- Digital technology and AI—promise, potential and reality
- Peace, harmony and collective values.

3.2 Censorship and Today's 'Anti-woke' Movement

Censorship is by no means a new phenomenon and can be identified in both authoritarian and democratic states. At times it takes a strongly moral tone as shown by Hilliard (1921) in his review of Great Britain from the mid-nineteenth onwards. He showed that while attitudes slowly changed to issues such as gender and sexuality it was often a slow battle with entrenched groups wishing to maintain the status quo rather than accept new ways of thinking. This even extended to the state's role in banning books such as *Lady Chatterley's Lover* that were seen to offend community standards of the day. This fight on the part of some members of society to maintain a single standard of moral rectitude has not ended, as will be shown later in this section. Alongside it, however, is an additional kind of censorship related to politics and ideology suggesting that freedom of expression is under attack from multiple perspectives.

The Committee to Protect Journalists (2019) reported what it called the top ten countries supporting political censorship: Eritrea, North Korea, Turkmenistan, Saudi Arabia, China, Vietnam, Iran, Equatorial Guinea, Belarus and Cuba. Sometimes this involved restricting access to the internet and social media, imprisonment of

3.2 Censorship and Today's 'Anti-woke' Movement

journalists, surveillance and the development of laws limiting press freedom. Yet as Marthoz and Gibson (2023) pointed out, the European Union (EU), better known for its commitment to democratic values, also experienced problems with censorship:

> Maltese journalist Daphne Caruana Galizia and Slovak journalist Ján Kuciak (were) murdered in connection with their work. Other journalists had been censored, spied upon, harassed online, overwhelmed with disinformation, subjected to abusive lawsuits, charged with revealing state secrets, beaten while covering street protests, banned from public meetings, or lambasted by politicians.

The EU has not been helped by the presence of illiberal democracies such as Hungary and, for a time, Poland. The political impetus of these regimes is always to preserve power through managing information and allowing access only where it suits their purposes. Marthoz and Gibson (2023) are critical of the lack of action by the EU against the leaders of these regimes. The assumption seems to be that democracy should triumph over the infringements of authoritarianism. Yet there is a naivety here about the very assumptions of censorship that are rarely addressed. It comes to a definition of how we understand the purposes of censorship, both now and in the past. Jansen (1991) provided an instructive definition:

> My definition of the term encompasses all socially structured proscriptions or prescriptions which inhibit or prohibit dissemination of ideas, information, images, and other messages through a society's channels of communication whether these obstructions are secured by political, economic, religious, or other systems of authority. It includes both overt and covert proscriptions and prescriptions. (p. 221)

For our purposes, what is important here is the control function of censorship. Certain ideas, whether moral or political or social, are prohibited by authorities or individuals. There is an argument that this control or regulative function of censorship is not its most important characteristic (Freshwater, 2004). Drawing on a Foucauldian perspective, she argued that censorship can create new discourses around whatever it is that has been prohibited. That is, censorship also has a constitutive as well as a regulative function. Yet both she and Foucault have missed the point: regulation first extinguishes ideas before any process of new discourses around the prohibited idea can start. The constitutive function may well create a new discourse, but it will not necessarily reinstate the original idea, especially where state power is being used to extinguish it. As Freshwater (2004) noted, "it does not reflect the experience of censorship as the unwelcome imposition of external constraint" (p. 233). In terms of preparing for disruptions, the extinguishing of ideas is a counterproductive to finding much needed solutions for solving disruptions' problems.

Censorship can be discussed in these theoretical terms and Freshwater's (2004) chapter is a good example of such speculation. In such cases, the audience self-defines itself as within the academy where word play and theory dominate discourses. In the world outside the academy, however, there are real examples of censorship that irrespective of theoretical flavour influence the daily lives of citizens. Nowhere is this truer in the present context than with the emergence of the 'woke' curriculum that seeks to expunge certain ideas from the school curriculum—ideas that some in the community think are not fit for young people's education. There may well be a new discourse constituted around 'being woke', but the reality for many schools is that ideas and books are being expunged. We need to understand this new form of censorship and its potential for eliminating important ideas at exactly the time when we need as many ideas as possible to combat disruption.

President Barack Obama himself entered the debate on 'woke' culture, yet perhaps not on the side that might be expected (BBC, 2019). He criticized young people for being too readily "judgemental" on issues related to diversity, equality and equity. He seemed to reject the idea that calling out recalcitrants in the name of social justice served any purpose. While many accepted this critique, and even welcomed it, others were less sanguine arguing "old, powerful people often seem to be more upset by online criticism than they are by injustice" (Owens, 2019). The journalist went on:

> The issues that my fellow millennials, along with even younger people in Gen Z, tend to be "judgmental" about are the same ones many of our parents and grandparents have been debating for decades. Being outspoken about climate change, women's rights, racial justice, LGBTQ inclusivity and gun control — and critical of those who stand in the way of progress on these issues — is work that's been left to us…. we're trying to push back against the bullies — influential people who have real potential to cause harm, or have already caused it.

Obama's comments were part of a media report, and he is nothing if not a superb media performer. There has been very little academic follow up to push him on exactly what he meant so we are left with the bare bones of his comments as reported. Yet it seems he may have underestimated the depth of feeling about being 'woke'. This was especially among young people and groups in society who felt constantly under pressure on account of their values, their colour, their gender or their sexuality. For some, being 'woke' was a badge of honour. It was this status that in no small way eventually led to the 'anti-woke' movement. Obama cannot really be placed among this latter group, but his misunderstanding of the issue suggests that on this occasion his political instincts had let him down. There were others, however, who held a much more positive view of what it meant to be 'woke' and its importance to creating a socially just society.

A number of writers has made attempts to review the origins of being 'woke' along with the implications for society as a whole and education in particular (Caldera, 2018; Madigan, 2023). Adhikari (2023) put it this way:

> The term "woke" originally emerged as African American Vernacular English (AAVE) in the 20th century, where it referred to heightened awareness of social and political injustices, especially concerning racial discrimination. Over time, the word's usage evolved, and "woke" became synonymous with social awareness, empathy, and a commitment to challenging systemic oppression.

While this can be seen as a macro level approach to social justice and action, Caldera (2018), among others, showed how it had immediate implications for classrooms and the development of socially aware and civically active students. Under 'woke' culture young people were being educated to call out injustice and discrimination, a natural objective for democratic civic education and for democracy in general. What was more, 'woke' culture gained further traction under the Black

3.2 Censorship and Today's 'Anti-woke' Movement

Lives Movement (BLM), that emerged in the aftermath of police brutality against black men, and the MeToo movement that encouraged women to speak out against sexual harassment and other forms of misogyny.

In response, however, it did not take long for 'anti-woke' advocates to emerge seeking to censor these foci on social justice and restore white hegemony in the nation's schools. Often these voices were linked to power, so the yoking of power and censorship once again has become a dominant theme. González and Schiff (2024) showed how an anti-woke agenda developed to the point where "divisive concepts" such as critical race theory (CRT) or LGBTIQ issues were banned not only as part of Donald Trump's rhetoric, but in laws and regulations at different levels prohibiting discussion such as those. While the origin of discourses on anti-wokeness originated in the United States, they can also be found globally always aligned with right-wing conservative politics. Yet these discourses also move beyond politics, as shown with the use of the legal system to secure anti-woke ends. A good example is the state of Florida in the United States.

González and Schiff (2024) highlighted several sets of Florida's laws:

> H.B. 7 makes it an act of discrimination to "espouse, promote, advance, inculcate, or compel" a public-school student or employee to believe any of eight distinct concepts.164 Florida law permits any person aggrieved by a violation of H.B. 7 to sue for equitable relief.165 The banned concepts include affirmative action166 and any view that inflicts white "guilt, anguish or other . . . psychological distress. (p. 32)

> H.B. 1557—officially titled "Parental Rights in Education"—is colloquially known as the "Don't Say Gay Law."174 The law prohibits discussion of or instruction on sexual orientation or gender identity "in kindergarten through grade 3 or in a manner that is not age appropriate or developmentally appropriate. (p. 33)

The use of state power in this way shows that those in power believe two things: first, they have the right to sanction the knowledge to which people can have access and second, they have no compunction in using their power to ensure their personal views are translated into legal controls. This is the essence of censorship, but the problem it creates in the age of disruptions goes beyond the actual censorship itself.

There is a key issue in taking personal views and turning them into legal prescriptions for other people: it does not just supress ideas as ordinary censorship does, it makes them illegal. Individuals are entitled to hold such views: but what is their warrant for imposing those views on others? This is particularly so in the case described above where children are being deprived of knowledge because some people do not like that knowledge. In times of disruption, we need access to as much knowledge as possible in order to solve problems and find solutions. It is also of interest to notice the extent of this legal suppression of knowledge.

Lundius (2024) reported on an anti-woke conference held in London by the *Alliance for Responsible Citizenship. The agenda was clear:*

> Conservative and liberal speakers were critical of what they considered to be a failed liberal social order, fomenting climate alarmism, totalitarianism, "cultural Marxism", and lack of parental responsibility.

> Climate change was not dismissed, but reporting on its dangers were described as misleading and dishonest. The climate change activist Greta Thunberg was described as suffering

from a "histrionic personality disorder" and it was declared that the climate movement had similarities to narcissism and hysteria.

This shows that the anti-woke agenda is broad, going beyond proscriptions for school education and in addition proscribing thinking in those areas of greatest threat to the future. Its biggest danger is not that it questions new ideas, but like the Florida anti-woke laws, it denigrates them and seeks to expunge them. This kind of ideology does not help education and will not help to address pressing problems of the future. Censorship in future will be one of the biggest barriers to solving problems associated with the inevitable disruptions. This will be particularly so if power resides with those who believe only in their own insights and values and let these override what is needed for society as a whole. Overcoming such censorship will be a significant challenge to confronting our disruptive futures.

3.3 Nationalism, Patriotism and Love for Country

An important issue in the preceding section was the role of state power in enforcing censorship in schools and throughout society. This regulative function of the state can be compared to its more positive role looking after the welfare and rights of citizens, providing social services, education, social protection and economic growth. Despite these functions, or perhaps because of them, the state itself cannot be regarded as neutral. Weber (1946) defined the state as "a human community that (successfully) claims the monopoly of the legitimate use of physical force within a given territory" (p. 1). Marx (1848) argued in *The Communist Manifesto* that "the executive of the modern state is but a committee for managing the common affairs of the whole bourgeoisie". Foucault, on the other hand, rejected any general theory of the state "regard(ing) (it) as a relational ensemble and treat(ing) governmentality as a set of practices and strategies, governmental projects and modes of calculation, that operate on the something called the state. This 'something' is terrain of a non-essentialized set of political relations, however, rather than a universal, fixed, unchanging phenomenon" (Jessop, p. 6). While these are disparate approaches to understanding the nature and functions of the state, they have one thing in common: the state in either its essentialized form (Weber and Marx) or non-essentialized form (Foucault) is a primary focus for the location of power. How the state, or in Foucault's view, agents of governmentality within the state exercise that power will be guided by the principles of the political system and the values these impose on those who have access to that power. Given this power, relevant questions for this book are how it might be used for protecting that power and how can protective mechanisms enable the state to use its power to confront future disruptions?

Why would the state want to protect itself? The capacity of the state is unlimited. In Weberian terms, it has at its disposal military forces, the police, security agencies, legislatures, courts and an immense number of public servants employed to carry out its will as expressed in the political system of the day. There has been a long-standing debate about the extent to which the state should be part of the lives of their citizens with some, the free marketeers, arguing for less state intervention and others, supporters of a welfare state, arguing for maximum participation especially to support those who are the less fortunate in society. Jessop (2007) argued that the power of the state should not rest on "direct or immediate coercion" (p. 4) but should rely on its legitimacy. Yet he also pointed out "that organized coercion is a legitimate last resort in enforcing decisions" (p. 4). It is the tension between coercion and legitimacy that is the greatest concern in the context of this book. When the state seeks to protect itself is this simply a part of its claim to legitimacy or is it a coercive strategy? This issue will be explored in the remainder of this section.

3.3.1 Protecting the State—Assessing the Implications of Nationalism and Patriotism as Protective Tools

Nationalism. Russia's invasion of Ukraine in February 2022 is the last in a long line of European states seeking to legitimize aggression and using the power of the state to do so—weapons production, military conscription, elimination of opposition and the development of a public narrative justifying the invasion. On the other side, as Knott (2022) pointed out:

> Ukraine—a democratic nation-state—is fighting for its right to exist against a Russian invasion. Ukrainians are fighting and mobilising as citizens for the right of their democratic nation-state to exist, just as Ukrainians protested in 2004 during the Orange Revolution for free and fair elections and in 2013–2014 at Euromaidan for dignity and against corruption. (p. 46)

Knott (2022) explained this opposition in terms of "existential nationalism" (p. 46) on both sides. Ukraine believes it has the right to exist and will fight for that right. For Russia it is the opposite, believing it can, and indeed should, extinguish that right. While each country is driven by nationalism, morality is clearly on the side of the defender rather than the aggressor. This view is supported by the majority of European nations and the United States and is an important one to keep in mind in case. Yet that view should not mask the destructive nature of nationalism on both sides of the aggression.

Such nationalism, unfortunately not new to Europe or the world, eats up resources that should be focused on dealing with issues of disruption. This is not to mention the personal and social tragedies that are the inevitable result of the conflict or the global tensions created on a daily basis as Russia builds links with similarly minded authoritarian states and the Western alliance continues to support Ukraine's right to exist. Nationalism, the creation of the nineteenth century, is wreaking havoc in the twenty-first century as though there was no more important issue in the world than Vladimir Putin's dream of a new Russian empire (Florea, 2022). It is the power of the state that has allowed him to do this. Yet, in the end, lack of attention to more significant issues of disruption will undermine any dream he has of a 'new' Russia resembling its historical forebears. Nationalism is at best a distraction and at worst a delusion. It can be regarded as a disruption itself and is not just negative but poisonous in regard to the real needs of the twenty-first century.

It might be argued that nationalism's focus on the sanctity of the nation state is the natural outcome of the development of such political entities. Yet this argument misses a crucial point (Kosterman & Feshbach, 1989):

> Patriotism taps the affective component of one's feelings toward one's country, [...]. It assesses the degree of love for and pride in one's nation - in essence, the degree of attachment to the nation. The Nationalism vector, in comparison, reflects a perception of national superiority and an orientation toward national dominance. (p. 271)

The distinction between patriotism and nationalism drawn here is common, although not agreed to by everyone in the field (Palumbo, 2009). Its value is in highlighting the destructive nature of nationalism that involves comparisons and the assertion of "superiority" and "dominance" of one country over the other. Vladimir Putin, therefore, is not just waging war. His "existential nationalism" gives him a sense of superiority to dominate those he considers inferior. This is why nationalism's return in the twenty-first century is so regrettable echoing Germany's Nazism and Japan's militarism of the twentieth century. Individual nation states seeking to protect themselves in this way only do so by creating destruction and damage. Given the central role of nation states in the lives of individuals, however, an alternative to nationalism is needed to ensure the nation state plays a constructive rather than destructive role in future. In the Kosterman and Feshbach's (1989) quote above, patriotism is contrasted with nationalism and appears to be more positive. Is there a role for patriotism, as contrasted with nationalism, in assisting nation states confront future challenges?

<u>Patriotism.</u> Kosterman and Feshbach (1989)'s description of patriotism misses the point that there are multiple ways of defining it and contexts for understanding it: there is liberal patriotism (Soutphommasane, 2020), critical patriotism (Fairbrother, 2003), constitutional patriotism (Muller, 2007), cosmopolitan patriotism (Horvat, 2020) and Palumbo's (2009) categorization of "ethical, protective, hegemonic and jingoistic" "forms of patriotism" (p. 329). This range of thinking makes it difficult to assess the usefulness of patriotism in the current context, but Palumbo's categorization makes some useful distinctions.

Palumbo (2009) rejected the distinction between nationalism and patriotism as proposed by Kosterman and Feshbach (1989) but instead identified forms of patriotism that were focused on a single ethnic or cultural group and the need to preserve these against intrusion from non-members. "Protective patriotism" (pp. 329–330) was one such form that sought to protect economic benefits and cultural values of a single group while "jingoistic patriotism" (p. 330) went a step further by declaring that a particular ethnic or cultural group was superior to all others and advocated the need to take whatever action necessary to preserve this superiority. "Hegemonic patriotism" (pp. 330–331) is not dissimilar from the other two types except in as much as it places a very high value on the ingroup and its cultural values and insists

3.3 Nationalism, Patriotism and Love for Country

that all other groups must assimilate in order to remain part of the broader society. This form of patriotism maintains the 'them'–'us' distinction as in the other forms discussed earlier, but its focus is on the cultural values attached to them and the need to preserve these.

These forms of patriotism—or what Palumbo called "patriotic identification" (p. 322) —are as destructive as nationalism in the sense that they insist on a division between an ingroup ('us') and an 'outgroup' (them). While much is made of the differences between the different forms of identification, the existence of any form of 'them'–us' dichotomy renders them ineffective in ensuring a socially cohesive approach to combatting disruptions. This distinction is also true of nationalism because the 'them'–'us' is between nation states themselves.

Palumbo (2009), however, did not stop with these destructive forms of patriotism. He introduced what he called "ethical patriotism" based on "the development of a shared identity" (p. 331) and the achievement of "social solidarity" that excludes no one and includes all members of a particular nation state. This might be better referred to as 'democratic patriotism', although Palumbo (2009) does not use this term. Yet he does argue for "participatory forms of democratic engagement" as the basis of ethical patriotism and as a means to "fill the gap between the individual and the state" (p. 331). This is the first direct reference in his article implicating the state in relation to patriotism and it highlights a major problem with his overall analysis.

Forms of patriotic identification do not emerge *ex-nihilo* within a nation state. They involve the direct intervention of the state itself acting as a channel for directing such identification. Fairbrother (2003) highlighted graphically this kind of state intervention with reference to the People's Republic of China:

> The party (i.e., the Chinese Communist party) began a series of patriotic campaigns with the 1982 announcement of the "Three Loves" – love the party, love socialism and love the motherland. A comprehensive action program for patriotic campaigns was promulgated in 1983 and schools were called upon to implement programs of "patriotic education" codified in 1994 with the publication of the "Outline on the Implementation of Patriotic Education". (p. 10)

Some forty years later Xi Jinping, the current Chinese President, reiterated the same values as the foundation of the Chinese state (State Council Information Office, 2022):

> Love of our country, the feeling of devotion and sense of attachment to our motherland is a duty and responsibility of every Chinese. It is the foundation on which young Chinese in the new era can become winners in life. In contemporary China, the essence of patriotism is loving the country, the Party and socialism all at the same time.

While this call may be seen as characteristic of authoritarian states, its essence can also be seen in countries such as the United States. Flag raising ceremonies, the pledge of allegiance, valorization for those killed in national wars regular playing of the national anthem at public events and the discourse on 'making America great again' are all indicators of patriotic requirements and expectations from US citizens. Of course, there is a difference between China and the United States on this issue: dissent is allowable in the latter (for example, see Westheimer, 2009) but not in the former. Nevertheless, where acts of patriotism are legislated in the United States they have the force of law. There is not a single country that actively encourages its citizens to be neutral when it comes to supporting national values and political frameworks: the role of the state is always to garner support and compliance. The issues shown in this section, however, indicate that the way this is done will determine whether patriotism can be a force for good in relation to confronting disruption.

On the one hand, there is virtue in social solidarity and the capacity to develop support for major initiatives that need to be taken in the light of threats from disruption. Encouraging the development of patriotic values such as love of country can bring citizens together for common purposes. Including all citizens in the country's development irrespective of their origins, ensuring multiple voices can be heard on issues of concern and facilitating legitimate forms of dissent would enable patriotism to make a positive contribution to future development. Yet any form of patriotism that excludes some for the benefits of others will be unproductive and should be questioned. This two-sided view of patriotism makes it problematic as a future value. In its positive form, however, efforts can certainly be made to nurture it, taking care to focus on all citizens and residents with no exclusions.

3.4 Diversity, Racism and Discrimination

The concept of "no exclusions" is one that can be applied in many social contexts and in daily living. It could be applied to applications for housing, schools and universities as well as access to transport, swimming pools and theatres. The reality, however, is that exclusion has too often been a dominant social and political tool seeking to separate members of society. It is sometimes a structural feature such as in Nazi Germany that was built on the exclusion of Jews, apartheid South Africa, built of the exclusion of citizens on the basis of their colour, or the Jim Crow laws in the United States specifically designed to exclude Black Americans. Ethnic groups have been a particular target of exclusionary politics including the Rohingya in Myanmar, the Kurds in Turkey and the Tutsi in Rwanda. These structural forms of racism have often been underpinned with legislation and the power of the state, its police, its military and its correction facilities. This use of power supports Foucault's (1997) view that racism is a "mechanism of the state……the basic mechanism of power" (p. 254). Racism allows the state to make life and death decisions thus wielding the ultimate power over its citizens.

Systemic racism that separates citizens into 'good' and 'bad' or 'them' and 'us' is designed to divide societies. At the same time, there are processes that can exist as part of a racist system, or even where there is no such system, that also have the effect of dividing societies. These processes are called "racial microaggressions". Spanierman et al. (2021) defined as "subtle and familiar communications BIPOC ["Blacks, Indigenous, and people of color", p. 1038] targets experience during interpersonal moments when White perpetrators imply targets are inferior or discount targets' identities, experiences, or knowledge" (p. 1039). There is a strong suggestion in this definition that racial microaggressions are an aspect of critical race theory and there is a growing literature in the United States that makes this link explicit. What

3.4 Diversity, Racism and Discrimination   61

this means is that microaggressions should not be seen as one-off or accidental—they are part of system-wide social injustice. Microaggressions may not be part of an orchestrated state campaign as was antisemitism in Nazi Germany or apartheid in South Africa, but they nevertheless reflect local level values that undermine and ridicule some members of society on account of one or other random characteristics. Microaggressions reflect the unease of a society by refusing to recognize that equality can only be achieved with equity.

Carstensen-Egwuom and Schröder (2022) argued that inequitable societies are complicit in disruptions and are unable to confront them on behalf of all citizens with some exposed to more of the problems than others:

> The effects of global warming are not only to be expected in the future, they are already there; and they are especially felt by people in the Global South as well as intersectionally marginalized people in countries of the Global North. In this contribution, we follow this important impulse and argue for the need to engage with the current Planetary Ecological Crisis when thinking about how racism works.

Racism, therefore, cannot be considered as an isolated social practice, as devastating as it can be. Even when racism is systemic and orchestrated by the state, there are always intersectionalities that exacerbate its effects—class, gender, poverty, etc. Ecological crises add yet another layer to these intersectionalities, affecting people already weighed down. Thus, the impact of these crises impacts individuals and groups differently. If individuals are already experiencing racism and poverty, for example, their capacity for responding to initiatives such as decarbonization, alternative energy sources and other green initiatives will be diminished. Cost alone may be one reason for this but so too are the likely mental health issues related to constant racism, whether systemic or in the form of microaggressions. It is for this reason that many have argued that Sustainable Development Goals (SDGs) are at risk as long as racism is allowed to flourish (Ebron et al., 2023).

The negative impact of racism is so pervasive that concerted efforts have been made to eliminate it. In 1965, the United Nations General Assembly adopted the International Convention on the Elimination of all forms of Racial Discrimination and it came into force in 1969. Under Article 2 (United Nations Human Rights Office of the High Commissioner, 2024):

> States Parties condemn racial discrimination and undertake to pursue by all appropriate means and without delay a policy of eliminating racial discrimination in all its forms and promoting understanding among all races.

182 countries are party to this Convention indicating that it has broad global support. To keep its principles before the international community, 21 March has been declared the International Day for the Elimination of Racial Discrimination. It commemorates "the day the police in Sharpeville, South Africa, opened fire and killed 69 people at a peaceful demonstration against apartheid "pass laws" in 1960 (United Nations, 2024). The United Nations support for anti-discrimination is unquestionable but international conventions require action at the national level to ensure international principles become part of national legal structures.

Not all countries that are parties to the Convention have followed up with local legislation, but many have. Canada, for example, has developed an *Anti-Racism Strategy* and an *Action Plan on Combating Hate*. It has also developed specific strategies supporting First Nations People and Black communities. On the International Day for the Elimination of Racial Discrimination in 2024, the prime minister made a national call for a society free from racial tensions (Trudeau, 2024):

> Diversity is our greatest strength. On this International Day for the Elimination of Racial Discrimination, I invite everyone to learn more about what they can do to foster a more inclusive society, free of racism and hate. Let's renew our commitment to build a future where everyone is treated with respect and dignity.

In Australia, the Australian Human Rights Commission developed the National Anti-Racism Framework and monitors the 1975 Racial Discrimination Act that "makes it unlawful to discriminate against a person because of his or her colour, descent, national origins, ethnic origin or immigration status" (Australian Human Rights Commission, 2024). In the United Kingdom, there have been successive pieces of legislation designed specifically to deal with racial discrimination: The Race Relations Act, 1965, The Race Relations Act, 1968, The Race Relations Act, 1975, The Human Rights Act, 1998 and The Equality Act, 2006. These successive legislative initiatives were in response to the growing complexity of racist activity such as incitement and hate language. The European Commission against Racism and Intolerance (ECRI) "specialises in questions relating to the fight against racism, discrimination (on grounds of "race", ethnic/national origin, colour, citizenship, religion, language, sexual orientation, gender identity and sex characteristics), xenophobia, antisemitism and intolerance in Europe" (Council of Europe, 2024). ECRI's role, however, is advisory in relation to European Union member states. Local action is still needed to actualize ECRI's values and priorities.

Yet, despite international and national action, racism stubbornly persists! There is not a simple reason for this as shown in previous attempts to address the issue (Loury, 2019). Yet it is possible to discern some key issues:

1. An historical dimension to racism.

    Adolf Hitler did not invent antisemitism in the 1930s. He drew on a long history of antisemitism across Europe over centuries. Russia, Spain, Poland and France all experienced drastic anti-Jewish actions long before the development of Nazi Germany. Black racism in the United States, South Africa and Australia has a long history going back to colonial times. These historical experiences are likely not inherited, but they are a reminder of bitter historical realities that construct racism as a normalized social practice. Yet as Loury (2019) commented, "it did not matter so much what the ultimate sources of internal behavioral patterns were; what mattered was how they were to be reversed" (p. 7). Thus, the important work of national and local governments, non-government organizations and the United Nations and committed.

3.4 Diversity, Racism and Discrimination

2. 'Toxic' patriotism

Yet not all nation states are committed. While many have supported the UN Convention on the Elimination of all Forms of Racism, there are others that have deliberately engineered a gap between 'them' and 'us' within their national borders. These kinds of patriotism were referred to earlier as 'protective patriotism' and 'jingoistic patriotism'. While these are described as 'ideal types', they are currently very evident in many of Europe's 'new right' political parties, the 'make America great' movement in the United States and Brexit in the United Kingdom that sought to demonize immigrant and non-white groups as a threat to 'British' values. These highlight the importance of 'ingroup' versus 'outgroup' politics in which the values and characteristics of the 'true' national group are reified in opposition to an 'outgroup'. Such a view is exemplified in the rhetoric of many 'new right' politicians such as Hungarian Prime Minister, Victor Orbán (R, 2023):

> We [Hungarians] are not mixed-race: we are simply a mixture of peoples living in our own European homeland … we are willing to mix with one another, but we do not want to become peoples of mixed-race.

In the European context, the 'outgroups' could be Roma, refugees or immigrants. In the United Kingdom, they could be Polish immigrant workers or people of African, Caribbean or Chinese background. In the United States, they could be Latin American refugees and immigrants, Hispanics and even those with a long history in the country including African Americans. The original ancestors of the latter were forced into slavery in colonial times; their closer relatives were the subject of Jim Crow segregationist laws and, despite changing legislative frameworks, still experience overt racism as shown in the deaths of people such as George Floyd, Tyrone Nichols and Trayvon Martin at the hands of the police. 'In-group'–'outgroup' politics, which are growing rather than declining, ensures that racism continues to exert its negative effects on individuals, societies and economies.

3. Racism as an individual value.

Henry and Tator (2006) defined an individual's racist attitudes as "a form of racial discrimination that stems from conscious or unconscious personal prejudice" (p. 329). They also link individual attitudes to broader social political values and in particular to the existence of systemic or institutional racism. It is this link that is problematic, or at least that should be questioned. Can individuals develop racist attitudes in environments that do not reflect systemic racism? Some would argue that such environments are ubiquitous and therefore always influencing individuals. There is no clear answer to the question. Yet the situation highlights the importance of anti-racist education targeted at individuals through schools, families, community organizations and businesses. That is, there needs to be constant reinforcement of positive values to counter the pressures of both individual and systemic racism.

This is recognition of the powerful influence of social and political systems and the need to provide a counter in terms of positive values to support individuals.

3.5 Digital Technology and AI—Promise, Potential and Reality

Since the focus of this chapter is on the future and how education can help to cope with its disruptions, an analysis of the role of technology is essential. Education is currently dominated by discourses on technology. These grew during the COVID-19 pandemic that in many locations globally led to the abandonment of face-to-face teaching and the adoption of various forms of online learning. These involved platforms such as Zoom, Teams and WebEx that created virtual learning environments for students from preschool to university. Technology as a facilitator of learning is clearly important, but in the broader society technology's role is not always so positive. Yet even when technology is playing a positive role there can also be downsides.

Duraku and Hoxha (2021), for example, drew on experiences in Kosovo where lessons during COVID-19 were delivered through public television. They showed that "from the parents' perspective, during the period of isolation, it was observed that children had changes in behaviour, were scared (showed signs of panic), desperate, stressed, frightened, anxious, confused and passive" (p. 33). It is no coincidence that in the post-COVID-19 period the well-being of both students and teachers has become a global issue (García-Álvarez et al., 2021). The issue for the future is whether technology's benefits can be harnessed without incurring negative spillover effects.

The idea that technology is a 'two-edged sword' is by no means new, although it rarely appears in current discourses that are more likely to talk up the positive side. This can particularly be seen in discussions of the relationship between technology and employment. The key issue is whether technology is a creator of employment or is more likely to result in overall job losses. The answer is not simple. The World Education Forum's (2023) job report, presenting the views of employers, reported "large-scale job growth is expected in education, agriculture and digital commerce and trade" and "the largest losses are expected in administrative roles and in traditional security, factory and commerce roles" (p. 6). Thus, technology produces winners and losers. Even if overall there are new jobs, for job losers there will be no jobs unless they are transferred or reinstated (Hotte et al., 2023).

Artificial intelligence (AI) adds an entirely new dimension to the technology debate. On the one hand, with its subfields of 'machine learning' and 'deep learning', there is a clear emphasis on the link with learning. On the other hand, the view of learning is not traditional. AI is not about how we learn; it is about how machines learn. Machines can be taught to ask questions and answer questions drawing on large databases and mimicking as far as is possible human intelligence. There are applications across multiple areas of activity including economics, law, business, industries, governments and education, including schools and universities. Yet, like other technologies, the contribution of AI is not always positive. It is important to understand both sides of the AI debate.

Zhai et al. (2020) in conducting a systematic review of AI and education identified both its potential and its challenges. On the positive side, the review identified

3.5 Digital Technology and AI—Promise, Potential and Reality

positive AI's contribution in providing "feedback" to students, the development of "reasoning" and "adaptive learning" skills, (p. 9), "role play", "gamification" and "immersive learning" (p. 11). On the negative side, "cost", "lack of personalisation", "over reliance by students and teachers" and "focus on technology not learning" (p. 13) were identified. Towards the end of the review, the point is made that there is little research on the impact of AI on student learning—a fundamental issue for consideration in the future.

A review by Tahiru (2021) identified a different problem for AI that was beyond education. The point was made that while AI was well advanced in developed countries the same could not be said in countries that might be described as developing. This is the old problem of the 'digital divide' between those who have and those who do not. Arun (2019) raised an additional problem:

> …if privileged white men are designing the technology and the business models for AI, how will they design for the South? The answer is that they will design in a manner that is at best an uneasy fit, and at worst amplifies existing systemic harm and oppression to horrifying proportions. (p. 2)

She goes on to point out that in many countries of the Global South there will be concerns such as opportunity costs, the use of facial recognition for oppression, restricted access to information and its reverse, misinformation, and loss of jobs. Arun (2019) argues for the development of AI in context to meet the needs of local populations rather than tech developers. These are salutary comments that apply beyond the Global South. AI always needs to be context sensitive wherever it is located. It should solve local problems and respond to real needs rather than imposing 'a model' developed out of context with no consideration of the local environment. This raises the question of how appropriately developed AI can support emerging challenges.

3.5.1 How Can AI Contribute to Confronting Disruptions?

AI's capacity is its focus on 'learning' that draws on masses amount of easily manipulated data to address key problems and issues. This learning might initially be done by a machine that has access to the data, but eventually the output provides opportunities for others to learn. Where there is relevant data that can be harvested and subsequently analysed using machine learning techniques, there is the opportunity for powerful learning. Climate change is one obvious area where data can provide the basis for prediction by understanding the past. Cowls et al. (2023) argued that AI can "can help improve and expand current understanding of climate change, and it can contribute to combatting the climate crisis effectively" (p. 283)

Kanchan and Shardoor (2021), for example, showed how deep learning techniques could be used with massive amounts of Indian rainfall data to predict future rainfall. Singh and Kaunert (2024) highlighted the "role of artificial intelligence (AI) in climate-smart practices" that can support the development of sustainable agriculture.

Chennupati (2024) showed the relationship between AI and electronic vehicles and the role it can play in reducing carbon emissions. This is not the only area of AI's contributions to confronting disruptions.

Another area is disaster management. Venkadesh et al. (2024) showed how AI can assist in predicting disasters and then with resource allocation during disasters. Ouaissa et al. (2024) showed how AI can assist those who respond first to a disaster while also supporting rescue operations by providing real-time data. Crisis management will be an important part of responding to future disruptions. Harika et al. (2024) highlighted that the solution to crises often depends on the data available. AI's contribution is seen as its capacity to make sense of masses of data and provide feedback in real time.

Commentators are agreed that despite the positive uses of AI, attention needs to be paid to the ethical issues relating to everything from copy right of the data used to racial profiling that can result from poorly constructed databases. These are important issues that need to be resolved with proper structures relating to the governance and development of AI. Organizations such as OECD and UNESCO have been contributing to this debate (OECD, 2024). Given that such issues can be resolved, there is little doubt that AI, as the leading technology of the twenty-first century, has a significant role to play in confronting future disruptions.

3.6 Peace, Harmony and Collective Values

The twentieth century sought to dispose of war as a global tool. The war of 1914–1918 was meant to be "the war that ends all war". Yet just over two decades later a new war started taking six long years to end with the first atomic bombs used in Asia and a land force of over 150,000 in Europe. But still no end to war. Korea, Vietnam, India, China, Israel, Afghanistan, the Soviet Union, Bosnia and Iraq all experienced war at different times throughout the century. The United Nations, established in 1946 with commitment to supporting peace in the world, spent more time in peacekeeping operations and responding to humanitarian crises but failed to keep the world free from war. This history suggests we cannot live without war.

Nursultan Nazarbayev (2016), the former President of Kazakhstan, in an address to the Nuclear Security Summit in Washington on 31 March clearly identified war as a recurring part of human history as well as its debilitating effects:

> Our civilisation, by scholars' estimates, survived more than 15,000 wars, approximately three every year. Hundreds of millions of people died, cities and countries were destroyed, cultures and civilisations vanished.
>
> At the dawn of the 21st century, stunning scientific discoveries are being made and new technologies are being invented. The world is on the verge of the Fourth Industrial Revolution. Many horrific diseases are being successfully eradicated, but the virus of war continues to poison the international situation.

He reflected that "humanity hoped that the twenty-first century would herald a new era of global cooperation. This, however, may turn out to be a mirage". How right he was!

The destruction of the twin towers in the United States in September 2001 by a non-state group motivated by jihadist ideologies led to war with Afghanistan and then Iraq. The United States and its NATO partners stayed in Afghanistan for twenty years and the Iraq invasion, based entirely on false intelligence, opened the space for the emergence of ISIS and an almost permanent state of war throughout different parts of the Middle East. The effects of ISIS were particularly felt in Syria where war became a permanent feature. Syria was also where, in 2019, ISIS' claims for establishing a new and lasting caliphate came to an end at the hands of an international collation led by the United States. Yet this was not without extraordinary loss of life. Starting with the attack on the twin towers in 2001 to the final defeat of ISIS, the world was in war almost as though it was to be the signature of the twenty-first century.

Wars were not confined to the Middle East. In Africa, there were conflicts in Darfur and Somalia, although not as much international attention was given to these. In 2014, Russia's annexation of Crimea, a part of Ukraine, rekindled war in Europe. This was followed by a full-scale invasion in 2022. In 2023, Hamas, a Palestinian political movement, launched a full-scale attack on Israel and thus began the Gaza War that continues with recent attacks also on Lebanon. So, war and the twenty-first century continue.

War in its daily operations is itself a dreadful prospect for the soldiers who have to engage in it and the civilians who are directly affected by it. McKinsey (2023), using the Ukraine conflict as an example, identified flow-on disruptions from the war itself including "humanitarian crises, energy flow problems, food security, increased costs, supply chain, telecommunications and financial disruptions, increases in defense spending, cyberattacks, scale down in corporate activities and increasing geopolitical tensions". These flow-on effects are not necessarily worse than the war itself, but they are in addition to the war making it not only a disruption itself but the source of multiple other disruptions. The article ends with "the longer the war lasts, the more powerful and unpredictable these disruptions may become". This is not a prospect that would recommend itself to anyone. But what is the solution?

The best solution, of course, is to end all wars, even though our propensity for starting them seems overwhelming. A second-order issue, however, is whether, as a prelude to ending wars, we can create a 'peaceful generation' for whom war and conflict are no longer options. The idea is not new. Esho (2024) argued for the development of culture of peace, "the capacity to develop, move and transform a previously shattered history into a new one of peaceful, social progress for the greater good of the community" (p. 88). This builds on the United Nations' (UN) concept of a "peace culture" that promoted non-violence in all aspects of life as a key component. Ironically, the UN "dedicated the decade "2001-2010 as the International Decade for a Culture of Peace and Non-Violence for the Children of the World" (United Nations, 2024). To explore the possibilities for a 'peaceful generation', the following issues will be explored:

- Is peace education an answer?
- How important is intercultural learning?
- How flexible is the school curriculum?

3.7 Is Peace Education the Answer?

Speaking of the twentieth and early twenty-first centuries, Harris (2008) pointed out that "peace education has not really taken hold in school systems around the world" (p. 22). There are, however, strong commitments to peace education in a range of jurisdictions: Columbia (Pineda & Celis, 2021), the Philippines (Kilag et al., 2024), Japan (Kim et al., 2024), and South Korea (Lee, 2024). What these countries have in common is that peace education is a reaction to widespread conflict either in the form of war at the international level (Japan), internal disruptions (Columbia) or a specific problem such as national dislocation (South Korea). Is this the only way peace education can be developed.

Professor Hilary Cremin, who runs a significant postgraduate peace education programme at Cambridge University, argued that "moral and modern interpretations of peace are grounded in pax, the Latin word for peace, the absence of war. This concept of peace is deeply embedded within warrior ethics, fear and in/security" (Cremin, 2015, p. 3). By contrast Kester and Cremin (2017) argued that "peace education, by contrast, focuses on the transformation of educational content, pedagogy and structures to address direct, structural and cultural forms of violence (p. 3). They called this "Positive Peace Education – (the) presence of values, behaviours and institutions that prevent physical harm e.g., reverence for life; peaceful security forces; and conflict resolution education" (p. 11). They embedded this idea in multiple social theories including those of Galtung, Freire and Bourdieu. The problem for our purpose is that this heavily theorized discourse is about peace education in universities that says little about how schools and how they might prepare a peaceful generation.

Yet there are lessons for schools in considering positive peace education. The first lesson is conceptual. Kester and Cremin (2017), first, distinguish difference kinds of violence—"direct, cultural, structural and post-structural" (p. 3)—and show how these can be understood as aspects of both "positive" peace and "negative" peace. The latter is about the absence of different kinds of violence—"no physical harm, no injustice, no discrimination and little reflexivity"—while positive peace is about "explicit values, respect for diverse cultures, laws promoting inclusion and reflexivity". While these are primarily theoretical categories, Echavarría and Cremin (2019) showed how they had practical implications in a real-world context.

They studied peace initiatives in Columbia that for over fifty years experienced civil war that was ended formally in 2016. One result of the end of territorial conflict was the establishment of a formal peace education programme for schools and universities. Echavarría and Cremin (2019) pointed out that evaluations had shown that this programme was not as effective as it should have been. They then go on to explain what was needed and what they included as part of their own efforts in the local Columbian context. My analysis of the context they describe is somewhat different.

An important issue to highlight is the grounded nature of what was reported. The article is heavily laced with theory, but its essence is rooted in the civil war experiences of the Columbian people. Peace keeping/building activities brought the violence to an end. Territorial peace, therefore, is important, but the article does not highlight this enough. Rather, descriptions like "negative", "modern" or "technical" are used to describe the cessation of violence. These terms are pejorative, yet territorial peace of any kind is a major achievement in political and social terms and should be acknowledged as such. Yet Echavarría and Cremin (2019) did make the important point: "it is necessary to draw on a wider set of global peace families" (p. 319) to make an effective peace education. The end of war or civic conflict is a necessary first condition, but maintaining this security is only one objective for peace education.

To achieve broader objectives, Echavarría and Cremin (2019) offered multiple theoretical perspectives that can be used to develop positive peace education programmes that focus on more than territorial peace. Yet these need some scrutiny. The focus is on non-violence as a general process informing all interactions, a reasonable foundation for peace education. They highlighted conflict resolution, peer mediation, global citizenship education and human rights education suggesting that any aspect of the curriculum supporting better human relationships and deeper levels global consciousness is linked to the development of positive peace education. They provided multiple theoretical perspectives to support this view. But there is a question about how far peace education goes and the other disciplinary areas start. Can peace education be everything? I can see why peace educators think it should, but I think practical curriculum reasons suggest why it cannot. The curriculum implications for peace education will be the focus of the final section of this chapter.

3.8 Peace Education and the Curriculum

The school curriculum is about constraints—what to include, what to exclude, when and why. These constraints are on the one hand about technical issues, like time and readiness to learn. On the other hand, they are also about ideology, what different individuals and groups think is important. This leads to debates about which and whose history should be in the curriculum, how much time for mathematics compared to art, science compared to physical education, language compared to social studies, multicultural values versus national values, patriotism versus global citizenship, progressivist values versus instrumental values and so the list goes on. Amidst these ongoing debates, that are common across countries, the question can be asked: where does peace education fit? In a contested space like the school curriculum what will make way for peace as both a process and an outcome?

There is a wealth of literature that addresses this question and Table 3.1, while not a direct response to that literature, reflects the opportunities available for making decisions about the inclusion of peace education in the curriculum.

Table 3.1 Curriculum space for peace education

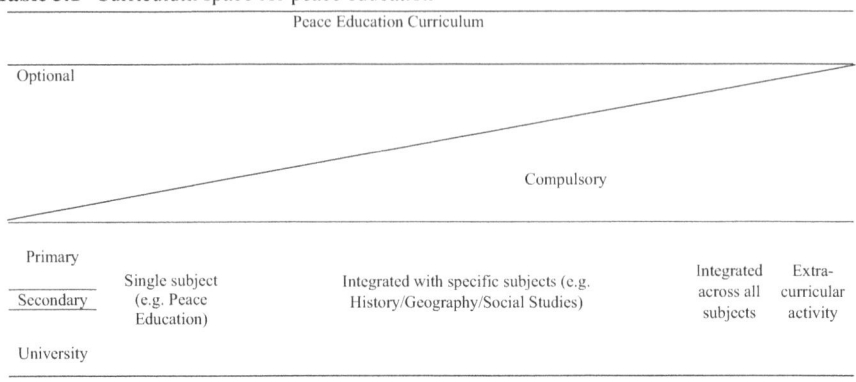

Source Based on Kennedy (2008)

Yet finding space in the curriculum does not provide a rationale—that is a local decision, and the literature is instructive. At times, these decisions will be affected by the need for territorial peace. This should not be underestimated, just as suggested previously in the Columbian case. At the same time, there are multiple examples of integrating peace education with existing studies, of effective pedagogical links to issues such as the Sustainable Development Goals and exemplars across education sectors from early childhood to higher education. Table 3.1 provides the possibilities for peace education.

There are, however, two key decisions not reflected in Table 3.1: the decisions to include peace education in the curriculum and whether it is optional or compulsory. These are policy decisions that can determine what schools can. At the level of the school and classroom, teachers are often able to provide much needed curriculum space. Yet in general, governments, their education systems and communities need to be committed to peace education for it to find a place in the school curriculum. Once that happens, there is little doubt that in its various forms and manifestations it can play an important role in providing the capacities to confront the disruptions that will affect societies in the years ahead. Citizens educated for peace are the most capable for ensuring a peaceful world.

References

Adhikari, A. (2023, August 2). The rise of "Woke" culture: A social phenomenon explained. *Medium*. Retrieved on 19 June 2024 from https://medium.com/@ang.adhikari/the-rise-of-woke-culture-a-social-phenomenon-explained-6ebdd8db67b4#:~:text=In%20this%20article%2C%20we%20delve%20into%20the%20origins%2C,social%20and%20political%20injustices%2C%20especially%20concerning%20racial%20discrimination

Arun, C. (2019). AI and the Global South: Designing for other worlds. In M. Dubber, F. Pasquale, & S. Das (Eds.), *Oxford handbook of ethics of AI* (pp. 588–606). Oxford Academic.

References

Australian Human Rights Commission. (2024). *Racial discrimination*. Retrieved on 19 July 2024 from https://humanrights.gov.au/our-work/employers/racial-discrimination#:~:text=The%20Racial%20Discrimination%20Act%201975,ethnic%20origin%2C%20or%20immigrant%20status

BBC. (2019). *Barack Obama challenges woke culture*. Retrieved on 18 April 2025 from https://www.bbc.com/news/world-us-canada-50239261

Caldera, A. (2018). Woke pedagogy: A framework for teaching and learning. *Diversity, Social Justice & the Educational Leadership, 2*(3), 1–11.

Carstensen-Egwuom, I., & Schröder, B. (2022). The planetary justice crisis, structural racism and sustainability education. *On Education Journal for Research and Debate* 13 April 2022 1–10. Retrieved on 17 July 2024.

Chennupati, A. (2024). Addressing the climate crisis: The synergy of AI and electric vehicles in combatting global warming. *World Journal of Advanced Engineering Technology and Sciences*. https://doi.org/10.30574/wjaets.2024.12.1.0179

Committee to Protect Journalists. (2019). *10 most censored countries*. Retrieved on 17 June 2024 from https://cpj.org/reports/2019/09/infographic-10-most-censored-countries/#:~:text=Eritrea%20is%20the%20world%E2%80%99s%20most%20censored%20country%2C%20according,China%2C%20Vietnam%2C%20Iran%2C%20Equatorial%20Guinea%2C%20Belarus%2C%20and%20Cuba.

Council of Europe. (2024). *European Commission against Racism and Intolerance (ECRI)*. Retrieved on 19 July 2024 from https://www.coe.int/en/web/european-commission-against-racism-and-intolerance/home

Cowls, J., Tsamados, A., Taddeo, M., & Floridi, L. (2023). The AI gambit: Leveraging artificial intelligence to combat climate change—Opportunities, challenges, and recommendations. *AI & Society, 38*, 283–307.

Cremin, H. (2015). *Peace education research in the twenty first century: Three concepts facing crisis or opportunity?* Retrieved on 4 August 2024 from https://api.repository.cam.ac.uk/server/api/core/bitstreams/44c9c6c8-64e7-49bb-8626-305e2fcd88b0/content

Duraku, Z., & Hoxha, L. (2021). The impact of COVID-19 on education and on the wellbeing of teachers, parents, and students: Challenges related to remote (online) learning and opportunities for advancing the quality of education. In Z. Duraku & L. Hoxha (Eds.), *Impact of the COVID-19 pandemic on education and wellbeing: Implications for practice and lessons for the future* (pp. 17–45). University of Prishtina, Faculty of Philosophy, Department of Psychology

Ebron, K., Luzynski, C., Komanski, C., & Caroline, S. (2023). Leave no one behind: How systemic racism impacts Sustainable Development Goals. *International Journal of Public Leadership, 19*(1), 31–44.

Echavarría, J., & Cremin, H. (2019). Education for territorial peace in Colombia: What role for transrational peace? *Journal of Peace Education, 16*(3), 316–338. https://doi.org/10.1080/17400201.2019.1697068

Esho, E. (2024). The paradigm of peace enhancing peace culture. *Journal of Aggression, Conflict and Peace Research, 16*(1), 83–97.

Fairbrother, G. (2003). *Toward critical patriotism—Student resistance to political education in Hong Kong and China*. Hong Kong University Press.

Florea, C. (2022, May 10). Putin's perilous imperial dream—Why empires and nativism don't mix. *Foreign Affairs*. Retrieved on 14 July 2024 from https://www.foreignaffairs.com/articles/russian-federation/2022-05-10/putins-perilous-imperial-dream

Foucault, M. (1997). *Society must be defended—Lectures at the College of France 1975–1976* (D. Macey, Trans.). Picador. https://cpb-us-e1.wpmucdn.com/sites.psu.edu/dist/d/37602/files/2016/01/Foucault-Society-must-be-defended14032016.pdf

Freshwater, H. (2004). Towards a redefinition of censorship. *Critical Studies, 52*, 225–246.

García-Álvarez, D., Soler, M. J., & Achard-Braga, L. (2021). Psychological well-being in teachers during and post-Covid-19: Positive psychology interventions. *Frontiers in Psychology, 12*, 769363. https://doi.org/10.3389/fpsyg.2021.769363

González, T., & Schiff, M. (2024). The uncertain future of restorative justice: Anti-woke legislation, retrenchment and politics of the right. *William & Mary Journal of Race, Gender, and Social Justice, 30*(1). https://scholarship.law.wm.edu/wmjowl/vol30/iss1/2

Greilinger, G. (2023, July 3). *Orbán, ethnonationalism and xenophobia*. Social Europe. Retrieved on 20 July 2024 from https://www.socialeurope.eu/orban-ethnonationalism-and-xenophobia

Harika, A., Balan, G., Thethi, H., Rana, A., Rajkumar, K. V., & Al Allak, M. (2024). Harnessing the power of artificial intelligence for disaster response and crisis management. In *International Conference on Communication, Computer Sciences and Engineering (IC3SE)* (pp. 1237–1243). Gautam Buddha Nagar, India. https://doi.org/10.1109/IC3SE62002.2024.10593506

Harris, I. (2008). History of peace education. In M. Bajaj (Ed.), *Encyclopedia of peace* (pp. 15–24). Information Age Publishing.

Henry, F., & Tator, C. (2006). *The colour of democracy: Racism in Canadian society* (3rd ed.). Thomson Nelson.

Hilliard, C. (1921). *A matter of obscenity: The politics of censorship in modern England*. Princeton University Press.

Hotte, K., Somers, M., & Theodorakopoulos, A. (2023). Technology and jobs: A systematic literature review. *Technological Forecasting & Social Change, 194*, 122750.

Horvat, K. V. (2020). Cosmopolitan patriotism. In M. Sardoč (Ed.), *Handbook of patriotism*. Springer. Retrieved on 14 July 2024 from https://doi.org/10.1007/978-3-319-54484-7_36

Jansen, S. (1991). *Censorship: The knot that binds knowledge and power*. Oxford University Press.

Jessop, B. (2007). *State power*. Policy Press.

Kanchan, P., & Shardoor, N. K. (2021). Rainfall analysis and forecasting using deep learning technique. *Journal of Informatics Electrical and Electronics Engineering, 2*(2, S. No. 015), 1–11.

Kennedy, K. (2008). The citizenship curriculum: Ideology, content and organization. In J. Arthur, I. Davies, & C. Hahn (Eds.), *The SAGE handbook of education for citizenship and democracy* (pp. 483–491). SAGE.

Kester, K., & Cremin, H. (2017). *Peace education and peace education research: Toward a concept of poststructural violence and second-order reflexivity*. Retrieved on 4 August 2024 from https://api.repository.cam.ac.uk/server/api/core/bitstreams/f13d9481-0e98-4844-a94b-442abcbcbb8e/content

Kilag, O., Mambaje, O., A., Rabi, A., Uy, C., Miñoza, E., & Padilla, J. (2024). The practice of peace education: Applied research on peace education in the twenty-first century. *European Journal of Higher Education and Academic Advancement, 1*(2), 82–91.

Kim, J., Hiromi Kawaguchi, H., & Kusahara, K. (2024). "No more wars": Peace education in Japan. In J. C. K. Lee & K. Kennedy (Eds.), *Routledge international handbook on life and values education*. Routledge.

Kosterman, R., & Feshbach, S. (1989). Toward a measure of patriotic and nationalistic attitudes. *Political Psychology, 10*(2), 257–274.

Lee, J. H. (2024). Development and implementation of peace education: Focusing on unification in Korea. In J. C. K. Lee & K. J. Kennedy (Eds.), *Routledge international handbook on life and values education*. Routledge.

Loury, G. (2019). *Why does racial inequality persist? Culture, causation, and responsibility*. Retrieved on 19 July 2024 from https://media4.manhattan-institute.org/sites/default/files/R-0519-GL.pdf

Lundius, J. (2024, February 8). *Is anti-woke a grass-root movement?* Global Issues. Retrieved on 21 June 2024 from https://www.globalissues.org/news/2024/02/08/35946

Madigan, T. (2023). Inverted totems: On the significance of "woke" in the culture wars. *Religions, 14*, 1337. https://doi.org/10.3390/rel14111337

Marthoz, J. P., & Gibson, T. (2023). *Fragile Progress: The struggle for press freedom in the European Union*. Retrieved on 17 June 2024 from Committee to Protect Journalists (cpj.org). https://cpj.org/reports/2023/04/fragile-progress-the-struggle-for-press-freedom-in-the-european-union/

References

Marx, K. (1848). *Manifesto of the Communist Party*. Retrieved on 10 July 2024 from https://www.marxists.org/archive/marx/works/1848/communist-manifesto/ch01.htm

McKinsey (2023), War in Ukraine: Twelve disruptions changing the world—update. Retrieved on 18 April 2025 from https://www.mckinsey.com/capabilities/strategy-and-corporate-finance/our insights/war-in-ukraine-twelve-disruptions-changing-the-world-update

Miller, R. (2018). *Transforming the future: Anticipation in the 21st century*. Taylor & Francis.

Muller, J.-W. (2007). *Constitutional patriotism*. Princeton University Press.

Nazarbayev, N. (2016, April 18). For a world without wars in the 21st century. *The Jordan Times*. Retrieved on 29 July from https://jordantimes.com/opinion/nursultan-nazarbayev/world-without-wars-21st-century

OECD. (2024). *AI principles*. Retrieved on 25 October 2024 from https://www.oecd.org/en/topics/sub-issues/ai-principles.html#:~:text=The%20OECD%20AI%20Principles%20are,human%20rights%20and%20democratic%20values

Ouaissa, M., Ouaissa, M., Sarah El Himer, S., & Boulouard, Z. (2024). AI and IoT integration for natural disaster management: A comprehensive review and future directions. In M. Ouaissa, M. Ouaissa, Z. Boulouard, C. Iwendi, & M. Krichen (Eds.), *AI and IoT for proactive disaster management* (pp. 1–16). IGI Global.

Owens, E. (2019, November 1). Obama's very boomer view of 'cancel culture.' *The New York Times*. Retrieved on 18 June 2024 from https://www.nytimes.com/2019/11/01/opinion/obama-cancel-culture.html

Palumbo, A. (2009). Patriotism and pluralism: identification and compliance in the post-national polity. *Ethics & Global Politics, 2*(4), 321–348. https://doi.org/10.3402/egp.v2i4.2002

Pineda, P., & Celis, J. (2021). Rejection and mutation of discourses in curriculum reforms: Peace education(s) in Colombia and Germany. *Journal of Curriculum Studies, 54*(2), 259–281.

Singh, B., & Kaunert, C. (2024). Harnessing sustainable agriculture through climate-smart technologies: Artificial intelligence for climate preservation and futuristic trends. In H. Kannan, R. Rodriguez, Z. Paprika, & A. Ade-Ibijola (Eds.), *Exploring ethical dimensions of environmental sustainability and use of AI* (pp. 214–239). IGI Global.

Soutphommasane, T. (2020). Liberal patriotism. In M. Sardoč (Ed.), *Handbook of patriotism*. Springer Retrieved on 14 July 202 from https://doi.org/10.1007/978-3-319-54484-7_44

Spanierman, L., Clark, D., & Kim, Y. U. (2021). Reviewing racial microaggressions research: Documenting targets' experiences, harmful sequelae, and resistance strategies. *Perspectives on Psychological Science, 16*(5), 1037–1059.

State Council Information Office. (2022). *Xi Jinping on patriotism*. Retrieved on 15 July 2024 from http://english.scio.gov.cn/m/topnews/2022-06/04/content_78252995.htm

Tahiru, F. (2021). AI in education: A systematic literature. *Journal of Cases on Information Technology, 23*(1), 1–20.

Trudeau, J. (2024). *Statement by the Prime Minister on the International Day for the elimination of racial*. Retrieved on 19 July from Discrimination | Prime Minister of Canada (pm.gc.ca). https://www.pm.gc.ca/en/news/statements/2024/03/21/statement-prime-minister-international-day-elimination-racial

United Nations. (2024). *International Day for the Elimination of Racial Discrimination, 21 March*. Retrieved on 19 July 2024 from United Nations. https://www.un.org/en/observances/end-racism-day

United Nations Human Rights Office of the High Commissioner. (2024). *Human rights instruments*. Retrieved on 19 July 2024 from United Nations International Convention on the Elimination of All Forms of Racial Discrimination | OHCHR. https://www.ohchr.org/en/instruments-mechanisms/instruments/international-convention-elimination-all-forms-racial

Venkadesh, P., Divya, S. V., Marymariyal, P., & Keerthana, S. (2024). Predicting natural disasters with AI and machine learning. In D. Satishkumar & M. Sivaraja (Eds.), *Utilizing AI and machine learning for natural disaster management* (pp. 1–23). IG Global.

Weber, M. (1946). *Politics as a vocation*. Retrieved on 10 July 2024 from http://fs2.american.edu/dfagel/www/class%20readings/weber/politicsasavocation.pdf [Orginally: In H. Gerth & C. Wright Mills (Eds.), *Max Weber: Essays in sociology* (77–128) [Translated] Oxford University].

Westheimer, J. (2009). Should social studies be patriotic? *Social Education, 73*(7), 316–320.

World Economic Forum. (2023). *Future of Jobs Report 2023*. World Economic Forum. Retrieved on 23 July 2024 from https://www3.weforum.org/docs/WEF_Future_of_Jobs_2023.pdf

Wynter, S., & McKittrick, K. (2015). Unparalleled catastrophe for our species? Or, to give humanness a different future: Conversations. In S. Wynter (Ed.), *On being human as praxis*. Duke University Press. Retrieved on 14 June 2024 from Books Gateway | Duke University Press (dukeupress.edu). https://read.dukeupress.edu/books/book/199/chapter-abstract/108242/Unparalleled-Catastrophe-for-Our-Species-Or-to?redirectedFrom=PDF

Zhai, X. S., Chu, X. Y., Chai, C. S., Jong, M. S. Y., Istenic, A., Specto, M., Liu, J. B., Yuan, J., & Li, Y. (2020). A review of artificial intelligence (AI) in education from 2010 to 2020. *Complexity, 2021*, Article ID 8812542, 1–18. https://doi.org/10.1155/2021/8812542

Open Access This chapter is licensed under the terms of the Creative Commons Attribution-NonCommercial-NoDerivatives 4.0 International License (http://creativecommons.org/licenses/by-nc-nd/4.0/), which permits any noncommercial use, sharing, distribution and reproduction in any medium or format, as long as you give appropriate credit to the original author(s) and the source, provide a link to the Creative Commons license and indicate if you modified the licensed material. You do not have permission under this license to share adapted material derived from this book or parts of it.

The images or other third party material in this book are included in the book's Creative Commons license, unless indicated otherwise in a credit line to the material. If material is not included in the book's Creative Commons license and your intended use is not permitted by statutory regulation or exceeds the permitted use, you will need to obtain permission directly from the copyright holder.

Chapter 4
Civic Values for the Future: Constructing Communities of Well-Being

Abstract There is little doubt that the future requires its citizens to see themselves as part of a community with common values and common interests. The polarization that has been such a common feature of twenty-first-century life cannot be allowed to dominate the future. In this chapter, multiple ways of bringing societies together will be examined in order to identify the commonalities that can encourage cohesion and collaboration, and bring societies together. This includes an examination of the Sustainable Development Goals as the most recent attempt to provide common goals for humanity and diversity and equity and inclusion values that have sought to create a fairer and more just societies. Issues of engaging in society will also be discussed with a focus on both political and social engagement. Finally, the importance of developing a sense of belonging and its relation to social identities and social capital will be discussed.

Keywords Community · Future · Diveristy · SDGs · Engagement

4.1 Introduction

Everything we do is underpinned by values. Across time and societies, however, there has been little consensus on which values are of most worth. There was a time in Europe, around the twelfth century, when the protection of Christian values and doctrine was seen to be so important that inquisitions were established as way to banish contrary thought in order keep church doctrine "pure". This involved public trials by priests and bishops resulting for some in torture and death by burning when those on trial were found to be heretics. Inquisitions of assumed Christian heretics continued in some countries until the nineteenth century.

The Catholic Church, both then and now, considered that its hold on the truth was so important that it had to eliminate all opposition. Today, the Dicastery for the Doctrine of the Faith continues the work of the inquisitions by protecting church doctrine, although fortunately its methods have changed. Yet the values of the Dicastery remain the same as they were in the twelfth century: protecting "the truth", as perceived by the Catholic Church, at all costs. We often see this played out today in terms of issues such as women's role in the church, LGBTIQ+ people and whether they can be welcomed into the communion, the church, birth control and abortion and transgenderism. Values are at work here and we may or may not agree with them, but we cannot ignore them. In the case above, values, or lack of them, could result in death. Values are central to every aspect of life.

Education is a value-laden enterprise, as was shown in the previous chapter, with different groups in different communities seeking to exert their influence. Arons (1984) argued that:

> Schooling is a form of communication between student and culture that inevitably contains moral implications, assumptions about the nature of reality, and beliefs about the most enduring questions of civilization and human nature.

Given this deeply value-laden process, it seems clear that alerting students to the importance of values should be part of their schooling journeys as well as equipping them with knowledge and skills. Yet does this require the teaching of specific values or is it preferable to teach students how to develop values? At one time, there was considerable support for the latter that seemed to reinforce the school's value-neutral stance. Yet it was not uncontested. Kirschenbaum et al. (1977), for example, felt the need to launch a spirited defence of what was called "values clarification" in response to criticisms that it was "relativistic, value free" (p. 744). The position taken in this chapter is that while a valuing process can be important in seeking to understand values and the difference between values, it can only be the first step in adopting values that can underpin 'the good life' in any society.

This chapter, therefore, seeks to identify values that may be described in curriculum terms as being 'of most worth'. In general, I shall refer to these as 'civic values' that can underpin the development of just and fair societies. Identifying values in this way raises an important question: how do we expect values to be adopted? Values inculcation should not be an option. We have seen in countries like Nazi Germany, authoritarian Russia and Islamic Afghanistan that inculcating values can be highly problematic, creating bias, unfairness and discrimination. Values clarification could be helpful, but its openness makes it difficult to see how it can facilitate the adoption of values regarded as essential. Yet it is not enough simply to identify essential values. Thus, we need to identify ways that facilitate the adoption of those values that do not rely on inculcation. We shall return to this issue at the end of the chapter because it is central to what can be achieved as part of embracing civic values.

In the remainder of this chapter, we shall consider a range of possible civic values, their potential in developing communities of well-being and finally how we can facilitate any communities' adoption of these values. This will involve:

- An examination of the United Nations Sustainable Development Goals (SDGs)
- Diversity, Equity and Inclusion (DEI) as elusive civic values
- Engaging with society
- Building social capital
- Developing a sense of belonging.

4.2 SDGs—The New Universal Values for a Fractured World

4.2.1 Planning for the Future

The precursor to the development of the United Nations' Sustainable Development Goals (SDGs) was a report from a "High-Level Panel of Eminent Persons on the Post-2015 Development Agenda" entitled, *A New Global Partnership: Eradicate Poverty And Transform Economies Through Sustainable Development* (United Nations, 2013). The Executive Summary started boldly:

> Our vision and our responsibility are to end extreme poverty in all its forms in the context of sustainable development and to have in place the building blocks of sustained prosperity for all. (p. 7)

The group then suggested what they called "five big, transformative shifts" (to achieve this vision):

1. Leave no one behind.
2. Put sustainable development at the core.
3. Transform economies for jobs and inclusive growth.
4. Build peace and effective, open and accountable institutions for all.
5. Forge a new global partnership (pp. 8–9).

They concluded that:

> Taken together, the Panel believes that these five fundamental shifts can remove the barriers that hold people back, and end the inequality of opportunity that blights the lives of so many people on our planet. They can, at long last, bring together social, economic and environmental issues in a coherent, effective, and sustainable way. Above all, we hope they can inspire a new generation to believe that a better world is within its reach, and act accordingly. (p. 9)

Yet this was not a traditional development agenda designed for "developing" countries only. Responsibilities for both "developed" and "developing" countries were articulated. The special responsibilities of "developed" countries to be both disciplined in terms of consumer and environmental issues as well as supportive of the needs of developing countries were highlighted. Together with the five "great shifts" shown above these became the guiding principles of the SDGs—a new set of universal principles designed to support not only individuals but the planet as a whole.

4.2.2 The SDGs—Values for the Twenty-First Century

On 25 September 2015, the General Assembly of the United Nations considered paper 70/1: Transforming our world: the 2030 Agenda for Sustainable Development with this Preamble (United Nations, 2015):

This Agenda is a plan of action for people, planet and prosperity. It also seeks to strengthen universal peace in larger freedom. We recognize that eradicating poverty in all its forms and dimensions, including extreme poverty, is the greatest global challenge and an indispensable requirement for sustainable development. All countries and all stakeholders, acting in collaborative partnership, will implement this plan. We are resolved to free the human race from the tyranny of poverty and want and to heal and secure our planet. We are determined to take the bold and transformative steps which are urgently needed to shift the world on to a sustainable and resilient path. As we embark on this collective journey, we pledge that no one will be left behind. (p. 1)

The paper goes on to list the 17 SDGs:

Goal 1. End poverty in all its forms everywhere

Goal 2. End hunger, achieve food security and improved nutrition and promote sustainable agriculture

Goal 3. Ensure healthy lives and promote well-being for all at all ages

Goal 4. Ensure inclusive and equitable quality education and promote lifelong learning opportunities for all

Goal 5. Achieve gender equality and empower all women and girls

Goal 6. Ensure availability and sustainable management of water and sanitation for all

Goal 7 Ensure access to affordable, reliable, sustainable and modern energy for all

Goal 8. Promote sustained, inclusive and sustainable economic growth, full and productive employment and decent work for all

Goal 9. Build resilient infrastructure, promote inclusive and sustainable industrialization and foster innovation

Goal 10. Reduce inequality within and among countries

Goal 11. Make cities and human settlements inclusive, safe, resilient and sustainable

Goal 12. Ensure sustainable consumption and production patterns

Goal 13. Take urgent action to combat climate change and its impacts

Goal 14. Conserve and sustainably use the oceans, seas and marine resources for sustainable development

Goal 15. Protect, restore and promote sustainable use of terrestrial ecosystems, sustainably manage forests, combat desertification, and halt and reverse land degradation and halt biodiversity loss

Goal 16. Promote peaceful and inclusive societies for sustainable development, provide access to justice for all and build effective, accountable and inclusive institutions at all levels

Goal 17. Strengthen the means of implementation and revitalize the Global Partnership for Sustainable Development (p. 13).

I have included these here in full because they represent a remarkable agreement between all member countries of the United Nations (UN). In a century marked by terrorism prior to 2015 and wars after that date, there nevertheless remained this consensus on addressing key social, political and economic issues affecting billions of people. There is a wealth of literature examining, critiquing, reviewing, measuring and monitoring the SDGs. In what follows, I shall review what I consider a key issue in the development of the SDGs and then their potential for success.

4.2.2.1 SDGs—An Alternative Look

When first introduced to the UN, the SDGs were simply listed as shown above from 1 to 17. Subsequently, they were displayed somewhat more picturesquely:

Source https://www.geospatialworld.net/blogs/geo-enablement-of-sdgs-for-boo sting-capability-and-better-policy-making/

Even presented as a set like this rather than a list there is a sense that the SDGs are more like silos than a set of interrelated and coherent policy goals. There is a considerable literature pointing to both the need for greater integration and the difficulty of achieving it (Breuer et al., 2023; Collste et al., 2017, Tosun & Julia Leininger, 2017). From a policy perspective, including resources, it is understandable that governments in particular would like to see more integration. Yet as Le Blanc (2015) pointed out the inclusion of cultural, social and biophysical goals makes this particularly difficult. At the same time, there is an alternative way to consider these goals. It is not so much about integration as about the centrality of one of the goals without which the others could well be at risk.

Le Blanc (2015) explored the relationship between the SDGs using network analysis for the purpose of identifying the possibilities for integration. He found a full range of possible relationships. The most connected SDG was No 12, ensure sustainable consumption and production patterns (SCP), that was linked to 14 other goals (p. 6) with the least connected goal being No 14, conserve and sustainably as the oceans, seas and marine resources for sustainable development, linked to 2 other goals (p. 6). The point of interest, however, was No 4, ensure inclusive and equitable quality education and promote lifelong learning opportunities for all that was linked to seven goals (gender, SCP, peaceful and inclusive society, health, climate change, inequality and poverty) with the strongest link being to Gender. Le Blank (2015) described the SDGs as a "political construction" (p. 14) but the establishment of links between the SDGs provided a realistic policy-oriented approach that was more likely to result in effective implementation. While the idea of links between SDGs as suggested by Le Blanc is important, and the scientific methodology used in his study provides a useful technique for both establishing and understanding the links, there is an alternative way to conceptualize the important links between the SDGs.

Quality education is identified as SDG 4, with the overall goal being to "ensure inclusive and equitable quality education and promote lifelong learning opportunities for all". SDG 4 has ten targets to be met by 2030. In summary, these are (Global Goals, 2024):

- free basic education—primary and secondary education
- equal access to pre-primary education
- equal access to affordable tertiary education
- ensure young people and adults have relevant employment skills
- eliminate discrimination in education
- universal literacy and numeracy
- education for sustainable development and global citizenship
- ensure inclusive and safe schools
- higher education scholarships for developing countries
- increase the supply of qualified teachers in developing countries.

These are challenging and important targets, especially when seen from an equity perspective. Yet in another sense the goal is narrow—focusing on formal education. Education has other broader functions to play that enable it exert a more catalytic effect. For example, there needs to be education:

- about the SDGs, e.g., what they are, why they are and why they are important?
- for the SDGs, e.g., how to develop them further, how to integrate them, how to measure progress on their development?
- with the SDGs, e.g., incorporating them into learning areas and informal; contexts, acting to implement them, advocating for them.

This broader function of education supports all the SDGs including SDG 4. It is fundamental to the success of the 2030 agenda and can be a powerful force to support individuals and governments to achieve fairness and justice across the globe.

4.3 Diversity, Equity and Inclusion as Elusive Civic Values

While diversity, equity and inclusion (DEI) are presented hear as a separate value set, they are also central to the achievement of the SDGs. The second half of the twentieth century witnessed the emergence of DEI largely as post-World War II values in response to the horrendous atrocities committed by the 'Axis' powers (Germany, Italy and Japan). The growth of DEI values can be seen particularly in actions taken by the UN related to broad areas such as refugees, gender equality, racial discrimination and social and political rights. As many countries started to shake off the heavy legacy of colonialism, their UN membership charted a direction for the future. Yet UN action in these areas did not mean change in individual member states. The United States maintained its discriminatory social and political systems, especially regarding the status of African Americans, Australia's indigenous population was not included in the census until 1967 and in 1948 South Africa embraced its harsh apartheid policy discriminating against all people of colour. Yet mid-twentieth century did mark turning point demonstrating law and politics could be used to mitigate the effects of socially destructive social processes. As the following cases show, however, the challenge has been to maintain the global momentum occasioned or this mid-century surge in democratic civic values. At the level of the nation state, however, there were different stories illustrated by the cases below.

4.3.1 Case 1—Support for Diversity Ebbs and Flows

In the United States, the Supreme Court's Brown v. the Board of Education decision in 1954 laid the foundations for the desegregation of schools. It was followed by the Civil Rights Act in 1964 that banned multiple forms of discrimination including on the basis of race. These new legal structures represented the possibility of a new start for oppressed minorities. As time went on, the values underlying these structures became dominant. For example, Bowe et al. (2023) argued that in the United States:

> Workforce diversity shifted from a legal perspective to a more of a value perspective after the 1980s in response to globalization and cross regional cooperation because it was considered a core strategy for the success of businesses and corporations. (p. 79)

In a similar vein, Smith (2024) saw the current purpose of DEI in higher education was to "build a model of how pluralism can work in the service of democracy" (p. 7), a purpose far beyond the legal intention of eliminating discrimination. That is, for both workplaces and universities in the United States, DEI morphed from the legal structures that gave birth to it becoming a *motif* for economic and political democratization. Universities and businesses shared a common value: the importance of diversity and the necessity to see it reflected in the daily reality of organizations. This appeared like a promising trajectory.

Despite this progress, however, the second decade of the twenty-first century has witnessed efforts to dismantle DEI on US campuses in the hope of "reversing the woke takeover of higher education" (Pidluzny, 2023). The ongoing discourse has put DEI initiatives in US universities at risk (Lang & Lee, 2024). This process gained further support from the US Supreme Court *Students for Fair Admission v. University of North Carolina (2023) and Students for Fair Admissions v. Harvard (2023)* that banned race as a consideration for admission. What started in mid-twentieth century as an embrace of diversity and social justice ended up in the second decade of the twenty-first century as a retreat into conservatism.

4.3.2 Case 2—Colonial History Threatens Multicultural DEI

Australia pursued a "White Australia policy" from its inception as an independent nation in 1901—an inheritance from its colonial history. This meant that from the beginning of the twentieth century only 'white' immigrants were welcome to Australia and this was legislated as the Immigration Restriction Act. As the National Archives of Australia (2024) pointed out "the aim of the law was to limit non-white (particularly Asian) immigration to Australia, to help keep Australia 'British'". It was not until 1975 that the Racial Discrimination Act was passed and it was 1978 when all restrictions on immigration were removed. A robust multiculturalism followed the removal of immigration restrictions. Immigration from Europe continued as a result of the post-war need for labour and new pools of immigrants were attracted from Asia. The first groups came from Vietnam at the end of the American war, a war in which Australia had been a willing participant. Opening up Australia to Vietnamese refugees in the 1970s, and subsequently students, marked the beginning of a more open and inclusive approach to immigration.

While the new immigration policy 'normalized' diversity as a value in Australian society, it did not create that diversity. In 1770, Captain James Cook, the English seaman and explorer, sailed into Botany Bay on the east coast of Australia not too far from present-day Sydney. This was not the first European contact with Australia but it proved to be the most enduring. Maynard (2020), a Worimi man and historian, described the initial contact between Cook, his crew and the traditional owners of the land:

> …when Cook and some of his crew went ashore at Kamay what he first called Stingray Bay and later amended to Botany Bay they were confronted by an Aboriginal man and youth brandishing spears and roaring their disapproval. Cook himself was the man that first fired a warning shot over the heads of the man and boy but received a volley of spears in reply. He redirected his aim and the man was recorded as being wounded before the Aboriginal man and boy withdrew. (para 2)

This initial altercation was not the last between the English colonists, who formally settled in Port Jackson (now Sydney) in 1788, and the traditional owners of the land. The first verified murder of an indigenous inhabitant was in 1794–96 years after English settlement began (Wahlquist, 2017). Throughout the nineteenth century, there were multiple massacres of indigenous people, recorded and verified up to and including 1930 (Centre for 21st Century Humanities, 2022).

4.3 Diversity, Equity and Inclusion as Elusive Civic Values

Discrimination of a different kind continued throughout the twentieth century particularly with what has been called the "stolen generations" (Wilson, 1997). This involved indigenous children of mixed parentage being taken forcibly from their families by the state and Christian missionary organizations in the name of creating a better life for them. There is an immense literature around this issue some of which label the practice as "cultural genocide" (Van Krieken, 1999) while others have sought to dismiss the historical record as fabricated (Windschuttle, 2009). The historical record concerning the "stolen generations" is indisputable (Jones, 2020) but evidence does not always win the public debate.

In Australia, there is a deep strain of historical resistance to diversity. It was shown from the first days of European engagement with the traditional owners of the land. There is equally a refusal to believe that the actions of governments can be labelled racist and that caring organizations such as churches can be complicit in this racism. Yet the history of Australia's English colonization, up to and beyond independence, shows that the diversity represented by the indigenous population has rarely been valued. There is little evidence to suggest that anything will change in future as indicated by failure of the 2023 referendum to give indigenous people a voice in the political life of the country.

4.3.3 Case 3—Religion Threatens DEI

In his presidential inauguration address, Nelson Mandella (1994) labelled South Africa as "the rainbow nation":

> We have triumphed in the effort to implant hope in the breasts of the millions of our people. We enter into a covenant that we shall build the society in which all South Africans, both black and white, will be able to walk tall, without any fear in their hearts, assured of their inalienable right to human dignity - a rainbow nation at peace with itself and the world. (para. 19)

This was Mandella's attempt to reach across the deep racial divide and paint a picture of the way forward that put the past behind the new nation and created a future of unity and diversity. The radical nature of this vision becomes clearer from an understanding of South Africa's early history and how, over time, diversity has rarely been valued.

4.3.4 Early History—Where Life Began

South Africa is home to the UNESCO World Heritage Site, the Cradle of Humankind. It is a paleoanthropological site (Makhubela & Mavuso, 2022) about 50 km from Johannesburg. It consists of multiple fossil sites (UNESCO, 2024):

> The fossil evidence contained within these sites proves conclusively that the African continent is the undisputed Cradle of Humankind. The nominated serial site bears exceptional

testimony to some of the most important Australopithecine specimens dating back more than 3.5 million years. This therefore throws light on to the origins and then the evolution of humankind, through the hominisation process. (para 3)

Saugestab (2004) explained that elsewhere in South Africa there is evidence of human activity at least seventy thousand years old. This evidence included weapons and engraving tools and rock carvings. Indigenous people were interrupted by Bantu immigration in relatively recent times—about two thousand years ago (p. 24). Indigenous hunters, herdsman and fisherman remained and often worked with the Bantu although not without clashes and at times outright war (p. 24). This picture, although scantily drawn, is one of growth and development not dissimilar from similar patterns of indigenous development in the pre-colonial societies of Australia, the United States and Canada. Yet Western colonialism, from the Portuguese to the Dutch then the British, brought a tragic end to such development:

> The early (colonial) encounters with the Khoe semi-nomadic herders of the Cape area, and later the encounters with inland San hunters and gatherers rapidly escalated from interaction and exchange into a tenacious appropriation of land, a process of gradual decay reinforced by epidemics, disease and drought…creating a distinct class of people in a position of permanent dependence, cut off from their traditional means of production and livelihood and barred from participating in the emerging, economically dominant, settler society. (p. 24)

4.3.5 The Death of Diversity

The colonial period—or periods—in South Africa is complex. Oliver and Oliver (2017) attempted to simplify or perhaps more accurately to normalize such colonization. They characterized internal migrations within the African continent, such as those of the Bantu moving south, as "unofficial colonization" (p. 3). Seen in this way the European acts of colonization by the Dutch and the English are just another stage in the 'development' of the country culminating in the declaration of South Africa as the 'rainbow nation' in the post-1994 period. This explanation glosses over decades if not centuries of racism and exclusion on the part of white colonists in relation to the majority of black and indigenous traditional owners of the land. Respect for diversity was never a value for Dutch and English colonists.

Oliver and Oliver (2017) recognized this, but in their assessment seriously underestimated the brutality of the apartheid regime initiated by the Afrikaner National Party as "nothing else but a next phase of colonisation of this country" (p. 8). Apartheid was much more than this. Motivated by a distorted Christian theology consisting of "a-contextual biblicist and fundamentalist hermeneutics" (Loubser, 1996, p. 332), it was orchestrated within the Dutch Reformed Church and was planning from the 1920s. Links between the church and the state were strong so the unwavering belief that "diversity" meant "separateness" became state policy. This meant that people of colour could not even worship together let alone express love across colour, send their children to the same schools or universities or have the same right to vote and be engaged in the political working of the state. The apartheid regime

4.3 Diversity, Equity and Inclusion as Elusive Civic Values 85

implanted by the Afrikaner-based National Party in 1948 led to the development of a cruel security state, the repression of black and coloured peoples and murder on a grand scale. All of this was in the name of a 'god' who demanded people of different races be separate from one another. The case of Nelson Mandela himself illustrates this point only too well.

In one sense, Mandella can be regarded as the face of anti-apartheid, although he was not a lone warrior. There was strongly organized community resistance through groups such as the African National Congress (ANC), the Pan Africanist Congress and the Black Consciousness Movement. Mandella himself belonged to the ANC (and its off shoots such as the ANC Youth League and the Umkhonto we Size, the armed wing of the ANC). He most likely stands out because of his eventual assent to become the first black President of a democratic South Africa. Yet this assent was neither automatic nor without considerable barriers being placed in his way.

As an opponent of the apartheid regime, Mandela was no stranger to arrest and engaging in activities designed to undermine the government. By 1963, he was on trial once again, this time with a number of other anti-apartheid resisters and he had reached the end of this road. Yet the trial itself, known as the Rivonia Trial, has been hailed as a landmark (Allo, 2015):

> Over the next year, South Africa staged on of the most stabilizing and gripping trials of the twentieth century. On 12 June 1964 Justice Quartus de Wet handed down the most anticipated verdicts of his career sentencing Nelson Mandela and seven other members of the ANC to life imprisonment. But the verdict of history was radically at odds with the verdict of the court. In the verdict of history, the accused were freedom fighters, and the trial a trail of conscience. Instead of ushering in a society cleansed of subversive elements, Rivonia became a constitutive historical event that catapulted South Africa's struggle for freedom and justice onto the international stage redefining and reinvigorating subversive activities. (p. 2)

Twenty-seven years later Nelson Mandela was released as the apartheid regime started to collapse and by 1994 he had been elected as South Africa's first black President inaugurating the first democratic government in the country's history. Respect for diversity did not come easily to South Africa. Subsequent history has shown that achieving equality and equity remains challenging. Yet the removal of apartheid at the very least provided an opportunity for a new future that is still being created and the contours of which still need to be developed for a fairer and better South Africa.

What can be learnt from these cases?

Valuing diversity has been a hard fought battle in the three cases. While there has been progress, the battle is far from won. Right-wing politicians in the United States continue to expunge their racialized history from classrooms and the voices of white nationalists are far from quiet. In Australia, a recent referendum seeking to give First Nations people some input into the way their lives are managed and regulated was defeated. It was defeated in every State and the Northern Territory (although not the Australian Capital Territory). This leaves First Nations people once again on the margins of Australia's political system. Despite its democratic transition, South Africa is still in a liminal state with the highest Gini coefficient in the world and "race based inequality is still a real problem" (Valodia, 2023). The acceptance of diverse communities with a strong sense of belonging and a willingness to contribute remains the goal: it must remain so, despite the odds that continue to be stacked against it.

4.4 Engaging with Society

Participation in the political life of nations has been a popular theme of writers from the time of the ancient Greeks. Linked with the emergence of democracy, writers and advocates such as Jean-Jacques Rousseau, John Stuart Mill and Susan B Anthony argued the importance of an expanded participation in the political system. The importance of participation has also been argued by non-Western philosophies. Ying (2021), for example, argued for the development of a participatory theory of Confucian democracy. Mahatma Ghandi's use of civil resistance against British colonialism showed the importance of mass participation in anti-colonial movements in India.

Yet political participation is only one form of possible engagement. Putnam (2000), for example, argued for the importance of social engagement and it has been shown that participation does not always serve democratic purposes (Wang & Kennedy, 2023). These different forms of participation (political and social) and the ideologies that drive (democracy and authoritarianism) will be discussed in the remainder of this section.

4.4.1 Political Participation

Unlike many of his contemporaries, and even those who followed him, Jean-Jacques Rousseau was a firm believer in universal suffrage. Oprea (2024) pointed out Rousseau's rationale for such support:

> Without universal suffrage within properly organized sovereign assemblies there is no way to know if people have consented to any law. (p. 209)

Participation, therefore, is the key to legitimacy. Rousseau argued that people are more likely to obey the laws if they have had input to their development and they should not have laws imposed on them. This assumed a form of direct democracy rather than the representative democracy that eventually developed in Western contexts. Yet for Rousseau participation was more than an instrumental process—simply a way of getting laws passed.

Dagger (1981) analysed Rousseau's view of the "general will" that was more about how to participate or make decisions. He distinguished between decisions based on private interests and those made in the interests of all citizens. The idea of 'private' versus 'citizen' interests invests a moral perspective into participation since "the purpose of the general will… is to provide a principle that will lead to just public policy" (p. 361). Because only what is good for all will be considered Dagger (1981) likened this idea to John Rawls' "veil of ignorance" in which "the individual blinds himself to his private interests" (p. 361) in order to make decisions that will benefit the majority. This ideal of participation was very much a reaction on Rousseau's part to the selfishness and self-righteousness of the autocratic monarchies he was so anxious to remove. Much of it has been lost in the later transitions to representative democracy, but it stands as an ideal, perhaps a romantic ideal, of how participation could work in a society committed to equality rather than the pursuit of private interests.

Since Rousseau's time political participation has played an important role in the development of democratic societies. Full universal suffrage has been implemented in most of these societies although always with a struggle so it could be as inclusive as Rousseau would have wished. The role of women as full citizens was eventually recognized, although in almost every jurisdiction the struggle was protracted and gains were slow.

Despite the struggle for universal suffrage, political participation is not a civic value that is always fully appreciated. According to successive International Civics and Citizenship Studies (ICCS), adolescents indicate limited intentions for future political participation in terms of activities like joining a political party or standing for office or supporting a candidate running for office. When it comes to non-conventional participation such as protests, students are even less enthusiastic than they are about more conventional forms of civic engagement. Intention to vote in future is often the most strongly endorsed political participation item, making it one of the key democratic values as perceived by young people. Yet reluctance to engage more fully with the political system is not only the preserve of adolescents.

Dalton (2019) pointed to a range of activities, not all that different from those about which students were asked in the ICCS studies, where participation was declining, including voting in elections. In the United States, for example, about two-thirds of voters turned out for the 2020 presidential election, "the highest rate for any national election since 1900" (Hartig et al., 2024). In 2016, the turnout rate was closer to 50%. Participation, while hard won, has not been an enduring value for those living in democracies. There are some possible theoretical explanations for this and also some examples of where participation such as voting fuels authoritarianism rather than democracy.

4.4.1.1 Theoretical Explanations for Low Levels of Participation

Political participation theory is driven by two distinctly different theories: civic republicanism and liberalism. Both theories may be seen as closely linked to democracy but they pull in different directions in an attempt to safeguard quite different values.

Civic republicanism. Kellow and Leddy (2016) provided historical examples of civic republicanism in multiple political systems. They highlighted the difficulties in reaching a single uncontested meaning of the idea. Peterson (2011) reviewed the development of civic republicanism and in particular its links (and disjunctions) with liberalism and communitarianism. Rather than traversing these multiple definitions, it is somewhat easier to read a statement by Sir Bernard Crick, who chaired the committee that produced England's first major report on civic education, *Education for Citizenship and the Teaching of Democracy in School* (Crick, 2010) stating that:

> We aim at no less than a change in the political culture of this country both nationally and locally: for people to think of themselves as active citizens, willing, able and equipped to have an influence in public life and with the critical capacities to weigh evidence before speaking and acting; to build on and to extend radically to young people the best in existing traditions of community involvement and to make them individually confident in finding new forms of involvement and action among themselves. (pp. 22–23)

Crick argued that this statement contained the essence of civic republicanism focusing on engagement, action, involvement and a concern for the public life of the nation. Elements of this approach to citizenship can be seen in some aspects of the politics of Ancient Greece and in some of the Italian city states (Kellow & Leddy, 2016). Cush (2016) argued that Rousseau's views often reflected those of civic republicanism. Thus, sustained active and concerned involvement in the political life of the nation has a long pedigree in the history of political thought. Yet it is not the only line of thinking that has influenced what participation means in a democracy.

Liberalism. In outlining the role of civic republicanism, Crick (2010) also referred to what can be seen as its opposite: liberalism:

> liberal theory (demands 'good citizenship', invoking 'the rule of law', good behaviour, individual rights and at its best moral virtues of care and concern for others, beginning with neighbours and hopefully reaching out to strangers. But it may stop short of demanding 'active citizenship'. (pp. 23–24)

In a similar vein, Vincent (2001) identified "the core values of liberal citizenship (as) autonomy, agency, individualism, liberty, rights, equality, justice". But it may stop short of demanding 'active citizenship' (p. 51). Fernández and Sundström (2011) put it simply, "liberal ideology is defined by its opposition to the "micromanagement" of individuals" (p. 363). Participation requirements within a liberal framework, therefore, are minimal. This minimalist approach is exacerbated by neo-liberalism that seeks even less engagement since for neo-liberals it is the market that should be given priority operating freely without human interference of any kind (Somerville, 2011).

The most useful way to view participation, therefore, is on a continuum—liberal and minimalist at one end, civic republican and engaged on the other. Both give rise to versions of democracy and both have given rise to radical versions. For the liberals, voting may be the only civic obligation on the agenda—this allows others to make decisions on their behalf while they live their lives working for themselves and their private interests. Civic republicans will always seek to influence the political system not only through voting but also through what might be called non-conventional forms of participation such as protests and demonstration. These ideologies can influence citizens and may account for actions, or lack of them. Such ideologies also suggest that citizenship education will not be neutral when it comes to teaching about participation—the alternatives outlined above are clear. Yet there is one other alternative that highlights the role of participation in societies not committed to democratic forms of participation.

4.5 Building Social Capital—When the Social Is Political

Wang and Kennedy (2023) surveyed adolescents living in the southern part of Mainland China using a questionnaire adapted from ICCS. The adaptation was important: advice from Chinese officials regarding the questions on future participation provided local examples that would be recognized by Chinese students responding to the survey. These were strongly endorsed by students responding to the survey questions. In the Chinese context, therefore, 'participation' meant 'regime supporting participation'. In both the liberal and civic republican forms of participation allowed for opposition to a regime whether by a simple vote registered for a political party not in office or by protesting directly against the government. The nature of the regime is the key issue here with forms of participation determined by values related to the role of citizens in the political life of the country.

4.5 Building Social Capital—When the Social Is Political

In ICCS, adolescents are asked two kinds of questions about their future and present participation. As discussed above, one set of questions is about future political engagement (voting, joining political parties, etc.) and the other is about social engagement (helping the elderly, donating money, supporting the environment). In one sense, these latter kind of questions can be seen to reflect a liberal view of citizenship—these social activities are what 'good citizens' are expected to do or they are activities that help to shape character. Yet social engagement has been conceptualized quite differently from this liberal conception and it is helpful to understand this broader conception.

At the beginning of the twenty-first century, Harvard sociologist, Robert Putnam, argued that "connections between individuals" in the United States had declined over the course of the twentieth century (Putnam, 2000, p. 19). These connections were what he meant by "social capital". Putnam (2000) argued that such connections were developed in organizations like Parent Teacher Associations, Rotary Clubs, bowling teams, Sunday school classes, youth groups, etc., the key outcomes being that "trustworthiness lubricates social life…civic engagement and social capital entail mutual obligation and responsibility for action" (p. 21). A society that is characterized by high levels of social capital is one where there is less conflict, more mutual respect and a willingness to work together. If, as Putnam (2000) argued, social capital had declined in the United States, then the dispositions he referenced were also in decline thus creating a very different kind of society from the one Putnam envisaged.

Putnam's (2000) position could not be further from the liberal view that societies consist of individuals who should be allowed to pursue their private interests. His view was entirely the opposite and it had developed over time. *Prior to Bowling Alone in America,* he had expressed his views on the political purposes of social capital development. He linked what seemed like purely social networks with political outcomes suggesting provocatively (Putnam, 1993):

how we might overcome the poverty and violence of South Central Los Angeles, or revitalize industry in the Rust Belt, or nurture the fledgling democracies of the former Soviet empire and the erstwhile Third World. (p. 101)

His answer was to develop social capital or networks that would draw people together, working cooperatively with a common purpose. His research on regional government in Italy (Putnam et al., 1993) showed two different kinds of development. One evidenced the creation of "civic communities" that worked away on their problems with government and community support. Other regions were classified as "uncivic" where there was little social capital and where individual interests almost always took priority over public interests. For Putnam, these two different approaches for development provided the empirical evidence for the positive role of social capital not just in bringing people together for social purposes but importantly for achieving longer-term political and economic goals.

Social capital and its underlying theory have had both critics and supporters. One such criticism was recognized by Putnam (2000): social capital can develop negatively, the Ku Klux Klan being one of Putnam's examples. In the current environment, we can cite in the United States groups such as the white nationalist Proud Boys and globally ISIS fits this category as do the various anti-immigrant groups in Europe and the United Kingdom. Putnam (2000) called these anti-social groups (p. 22) compared to the pro-social agenda for positively oriented social capital that he promoted. Over time more evidence has accumulated for the effectiveness of pro-social social capital. Durante et al. (2024), for example, showed how social capital was more multifaceted than a single dimensional construct and exerts positive health, political and economic outcomes (p. 1). There are now multiple studies along these lines in areas such as tourism, environmentalism, community resilience and entrepreneurship. These empirical results suggest that the positive role of social capital needs greater recognition.

4.5.1 Social Media and Social Capital

There has been considerable support for the role of social media in providing an alternative avenue for adolescent civic engagement (Kahne et al., 2016, 2014). Yet this view has also been contested by social movement theorists who insist on the primacy of face-to-face engagement and those who do not equate "clicktivism" with engagement (Kennedy, 2021). Very early on, however, Putnam (2000) had identified internet chat groups as forums for developing social capital (p. 21) rather than as a form of civic engagement. Over time, social media engagement has expanded from the idea of simple chat groups and has been associated with multiple purposes: explicit political objectives, conveying misinformation and political conspiracy, informal communication between friends and family and more. These different purposes have even greater potential for developing social capital but raise the issue of the role of social media

4.5 Building Social Capital—When the Social Is Political

in this process. What is the relationship between social media and the development of social capital?

Groups using social media are usually made up of like-minded individuals exchanging information and ideas. As Putnam pointed out, such groups have the potential to form connections as they communicate on topics of common interest. These connections may be pro-social or anti-social, but it is not social media that makes them so. It is the purpose of the group that will determine the nature of its outcomes—an anti-immigration group will likely create anti-social outcomes while a group set up to support refugees is likely to have pro-social outcomes. The various social media platforms do little more than provide a process for facilitating communication. This technology-mediated participation is the most recent technological development that is symptomatic of modernity. Powerful as it is, it does not have any influence on the nature of the resulting communication. Social media simply provide the platforms for communication—they are the medium not the message.

Participating through social media, therefore, is little different from other forms of participation. As the medium of participation, social media are certainly powerful in terms of their ubiquity, ease of access and popularity. But in themselves they are not the problem. It is the groups that choose to use social media that are the problem. If they peddle false information, hate speech and ideas not open to debate and discussion, their impact will result in anti-social social capital. Banning children's access to social media, as the Australian government is planning to do (Taylor, 2024), will not solve this problem. The hate will still be there and it will continue to confront children in their peer groups, as they watch television and in their communities. The bigger problem, both now and in future, is how to manage hate so that it is not a feature of modern life.

As disruptions come, there will be the tendency to place blame on someone or some group. History has shown that such a tendency usually focuses on the most disadvantaged: it is the fault of migrants and those who not speak our language, those who have a different religions and dress differently and those whose skin colour is different from ours. It is the issues of blame and hate that need the attention of governments and indeed the whole of society. Banning social media will not solve complex social issues that have the potential to exacerbate division and discord within communities—this is the role of communities themselves and their governments.

4.5.2 Schools and Social Capital

Putting aside the problematic issues related to social capital, and perhaps because of them, schools need to play a positive role in supporting the development of a pro-social and life fulfilling environment for students. This will be even more important in the future when disruptions will be a feature of daily life. Students need to face these together, sharing their understandings, their fears and their solutions and they need knowledge and skills for the future as disruptions continue. Every opportunity needs to be taken to build positive social capital among students to equip them for these future challenges. This is a lot to ask of schools that are so often in societies where division rather than unity has become the norm. Carnoy and Levin (1976) pointed out some time ago that there are limits to what schools can achieve when their aims conflict with those of the broader society. Yet the point to understand is that at the very least schools should not exacerbate society's problems. Schools always need to be part of the solution, often against the odds, but it should be unquestioned that schools must be on the side of students who represent the future for all of us. Chapter 5 will take up this issue in some detail since they remain key agents of citizenship education. Yet schools must be welcoming places and students must experience this as will be shown in the final section of this chapter.

4.6 Developing a Sense of Belonging—Relational Social Capital and "Communities of Circumstance"

Social capital creates the connections that bind groups and communities together, building trust through participation. As research has continued on both the nature and effects of social capital, researchers have identified a more complex multi-dimensional structure for social capital. Claridge (2020, p. 1) indicated that "identity and belonging are commonly mentioned as elements of the relational dimension of social capital":

> It orients actors towards shared goals, intensifies obligations towards the group or community, increases the likelihood of social support, improves collective efficacy, and empowers collective action. (p. 1)

'Sense of belonging' as a social construct has a long history of its own. Yuval-Davis (2006) provided an analysis based on the definition that "belonging is about emotional attachment, about feeling 'at home'… about feeling 'safe'" (p. 197). She identified three analytical levels of belonging: "social locations… individuals' identifications and emotional attachments to various collectivities and groupings (and) the ethical and political value systems with which people judge their own and others' belonging/s" (p. 199). As I see it the strongest link between 'sense of belonging' and 'social capital' is the second level concerned with people's identity.

For Yuval-Davis (2006), "identities are narratives, stories people tell themselves and others about who they are (and who they are not)" (p. 202). But these stories are not merely cognitive in nature but rather about emotion and attachment. She draws on Elspeth Probyn (1996)'s idea that:

> Individuals and groups are caught within wanting to belong, wanting to become, a process that is fuelled by yearning rather than positing identity as a stable state. (p. 1)

Identity building within community/national/global groups is likely a natural process that occurs over time as trust builds. But it is more than trust: it is the outcome of trustful relationships so that the deeper the trust between individuals the greater the process of identification with the group, its purposes and its actions. But, as has been

4.6 Developing a Sense of Belonging—Relational Social Capital ...

pointed out, identity has an even more important role in times of disaster. This is an important issue to consider in the light of potential disruptions in future.

Ntontis et al. (2020) pointed out with respect to the United Kingdom that social capital and its capacity to build networks had become an important part of public policy related to disaster management. While accepting the accumulated evidence suggesting the importance of social capital in disaster management, they raised two key questions:

> social capital cannot explain the mechanisms through which networks emerge and are transformed into collective action (and) … it does not explain processes of emergence— how unexpected social capital emerges and how communities engage in processes of collective transformation. (p. 260)

The focus on "unexpected social capital" is a key point being made here. It is referred to elsewhere in the paper as "communities of circumstance" (p. 257). The argument is that disasters create their own needs that are unlikely to be met by preexisting groups. Disasters, like disruptions, strike randomly, so affected individuals are unlikely to know one another and they are likely to be spread across geographic regions. On the surface, therefore, a basis for working together seems problematic. Ntonis et al. (2020), however, examined number of empirical studies of disaster situations and suggested some underlying processes that appear to facilitate emergent group formation in response to specific disasters. At the heart of their analyses was the identification of a common fate as a facilitating factor leading to supporting behaviours, in terms of both physical resources as well as emotional support, the development of a shared social identity and a willingness to continue to work together. These processes are referred to as "natural resilience" (p. 261). They seem to occur naturally in disaster contexts often having the potential to turn into "enduring social capital" (p. 260).

Naturally developed communities responding to disaster have a certain appeal about it drawing on the most positive capacities of human beings. Yet it leaves a number of questions unanswered. These refer to the nature of social identity, the ways in which it can be mobilized and the relationship between "communities of circumstance" and social capital.

4.6.1 The Nature of Social Identity

Ntonis et al. (2020), relied broadly on the field of social psychology, and social cognitive theory in particular, to formulate their understanding of social identity. They advocated in particular for the "the social identity model of collective psychosocial resilience" (SIMCPR) (p. 257). While there appears to be some flexibility in this model, its psychological basic underpinnings are cognitive in orientation. This make is different from Yuval-Davis' (2006) view that social identity is more of an emotional than a cognitive attachment that is not fixed in time. We cannot solve these differences here but given the centrality of social identity, more work is needed to locate it theoretically as a central concept in social development.

4.6.2 Mobilizing "Communities of Circumstance"

Ntonis et al. (2020) make a strong case for the almost spontaneous emergence of groups in response to disasters providing evidence collected retrospectively from specific disaster experiences. The issue, however, is whether this means we can always rely on such a process in times of disaster or do we need to prepare people for the eventuality? Their advocacy is very strong, "it is shared social identity that can act as the mediating mechanism through which community development can positively foster community resilience" (p. 26). Yet it remains an article of faith that social identity will emerge in response to contexts and circumstances. They have proposed a research agenda and this may help unravel more specific mobilization strategies that can facilitate the development of "communities of circumstance".

4.6.3 Communities of Circumstance and Social Capital

Ntonis et al. (2020) are critical of social capital as a tool to confront the issues raised by disasters largely because preexisting networks may not be relevant and therefore not applicable to specific disaster contexts. On the other hand, communities of circumstance emerge from those contexts. These emergent communities may well be sustained by social identity, but they are nevertheless forms of social capital. They are networks formed spontaneously for special purposes. I would call them hyper-social capital since they represent processes quickly formed in response to emergencies. Such social capital may well be the pathway to the future as we confront multiple disruptions. We need to know more about its formation and mobilization since the future may well depend on them. As disruptions emerge, more research is needed so that the role of hyper-social capital can be monitored and best practice can be identified.

References

Allo, A. (2015). The courtroom as a space of resistance: Reflections on the legacy of the Rivonia Trial. In A. Allo (Ed.), *The courtroom as a space of resistance: Reflections on the legacy of the Rivonia Trial* (pp. 1–20). Routledge.

Anita B., Leininger, J., Malerba, D., & Tosun, J. (2023, October). Integrated policymaking: Institutional designs for implementing the sustainable development goals (SDGs). *World Development*, 106317. https://doi.org/10.1016/j.worlddev.2023.106317

Arons, S. (1984, November 7). The myth of value-free education. *Education Week*. Retrieved on 12 August 2024 from https://www.edweek.org/education/opinion-the-myth-of-value-neutral-schooling/1984/11

Bowe, A., Drame, E., Derute, D., Mawhinney, L., & Melaco, C. (2023). Measuring DEI within workplaces: Questioning the theoretical, empirical, and practical models. *Bulletin De Methodologie Sociologique, 159*, 75–89. https://doi.org/10.1177/07591063231184252

References

Breuer, A., Leininger, J., Malerba, D., & Tosun, J. (2023). Integrated policymaking: Institutional designs for implementing the sustainable development goals (SDGs). *World Development, 170*, 10637, https://doi.org/10.1016/j.worlddev.2023.106317

Carnoy, M., & Levin, H. (1976). *The limits of educational reform*. D. McKay Company.

Centre for 21st Century Humanities. (2022). *Colonial frontier massacres in Australia, 1788–1930*. Retrieved on 1 September 2024 from https://c21ch.newcastle.edu.au/colonialmassacres/timeline.

Claridge, T. (2020). *Social capital at different levels and dimensions: A typology of social capital*. Retrieved on 27 October 2024 from https://www.socialcapitalresearch.com/wp-content/uploads/2020/08/Dimensions-and-levels.pdf

Collste, D., Pedercini, M., & Cornell, S. (2017). Policy coherence to achieve the SDGs: Using integrated simulation models to assess effective policies. *Sustainability Science, 12*, 921–931. https://doi.org/10.1007/s11625-017-0457-x

Crick, B. (2010). Civic republicanism and citizenship: The challenge for today. In B. Crick & A. Lockyer (Eds.), *Active citizenship: What could it achieve?* (pp. 16–25). Edinburgh University Press.

Cush, B. (2016). A master of the art of persuasion: Rousseau's Platonic teaching on the virtuous legislator. In G. Kellow & N. Leddy (Eds.), *On civic republicanism—Ancient lessons for global politics* (pp. 226–245). University of Toronto Press.

Dagger, R. (1981). Understanding the General Will. *Western Political Quarterly, 34*(3), 359–71. https://doi.org/10.2307/447216

Dalton, R. (2019) *Citizen politics: Public opinion and political parties in advanced industrial democracies* (7th ed). CQ Press.

Durante, R., Mastrorocco, N., Minale, L., & Snyder, J. (2024). Unpacking social capital. *The Economic Journal*, ueae074. https://doi.org/10.1093/ej/ueae074

Fernández, C., & Sundström, M. (2011). Citizenship education and liberalism: A state of the debate analysis 1990–2010. *Studies in the Philosophy Education, 30*, 363–384. https://doi.org/10.1007/s11217-011-9237-8

Global Goals. (2024). *4: Quality Education*. Retrieved on 27 October 2024 from https://www.globalgoals.org/goals/4-quality-education/

Hartig, H., Daniller, A., Keeter, S., & Van Green, T. (2024). Voter turnout, 2018–2022. *Pew Research Center*. Retrieved on 9 September 2024 from https://www.pewresearch.org/politics/2023/07/12/voter-turnout-2018-2022/

Jones, B. (2020). *Denying the stolen generations—What happens to indigenous history in a post-truth world?* Routledge.

Kahne, J., Hodgin, E., & Eidman-Aadahl, E. (2016). Redesigning civic education for the digital age: Participatory politics and the pursuit of democratic engagement. *Theory & Research in Social Education, 44*(1), 1–35.

Kahne, J. Middaugh, J., & Allen, D. (2014). *Youth, new media, and the rise of participatory politics* (Working Paper No 1). Youth & Participatory Politics Research Network. https://clalliance.org/wp-content/uploads/files/ypp_workinpapers_paper01_1.pdf

Kellow, G., & Leddy, N. (Eds.). (2016). *On civic republicanism—Ancient lessons for global politics*. University of Toronto Press.

Kennedy, K. (2021). *Civic engagement in changing contexts—Challenges and possibilities for democracy*. Springer

Kirschenbaum, H., Harmin, M., Howe, L., & Simon, S. (1977). In defense of values clarification. *Phi Delta Kappan, 58*(10), 743–746.

Lang, A., & Lee, J. (2024). Centering our humanity: Responding to anti-DEI efforts across higher education. *Journal of College Student Development, 65*(1), 113–116. https://doi.org/10.1353/csd.2024.a919356

Le Blanc, D. (2015). *Towards integration at last? The sustainable development goals as a network of targets* (United Nations Department of Economic and Social Affairs (DESA) Working Paper

No 141). Retrieved on 22 August 2024 from https://www.un.org/esa/desa/papers/2015/wp141_2015.pdf

Loubser, J. (1996). Apartheid theology: A "contextual" theology gone wrong? *Journal of Church and State, 38*(2), 321–337.

Makhubela, T., & Mavuso, S. (2022). Chapter Six—An overview of the geology of paleoanthropological and archaeological sites of South Africa. *Stratigraphy & Timescales, 7*, 221–268.

Mandella, N. (1994). *Inauguration address*. Retrieved on 4 September 2024 from Nelson Mandela—Speeches—Nelson Mandela at his inauguration as President of South Africa, Pretoria.

Maynard, J. (2020). *James Cook—man, mariner, myth or monster*. Retrieved on 3 September 2024 from https://australian.museum/learn/first-nations/james-cook/

National Archives of Australia. (2024). *The Immigration Restriction Act 1901*. Retrieved on 2 September 2024 from https://www.naa.gov.au/explore-collection/immigration-and-citizenship/immigration-restriction-act-1901

Ntontis, E., Drury, J., Amlôt, R., Rubin, G. J., & Williams, R. (2020). What lies beyond social capital? The role of Social Psychology in building community resilience to climate change. *Traumatology, 26*(3), 253–265. https://doi.org/10.1037/trm0000221

Oliver, E., & Oliver, W. (2017). The colonisation of South Africa: A unique case. *HTS Teologiese Studies/Theological Studies, 73*(3) https://doi.org/10.4102/hts.v73i3.4498

Oprea, A. (2024). Rousseau on voting and electoral laws. In D. Williams & M. Maguire (Eds.), *The Cambridge companion to Rousseau's social contract* (pp. 207–222). Cambridge University Press.

Peterson, A. (2011). *Civic republicanism and civic education: The education of citizens*. Palgrave Macmillan.

Pidluzny, J. (2023, 25 August). *Reversing the woke takeover of higher education: Strategies to dismantle campus*. DEI. America First Policy Institute—Higher Education Reform Initiative. Retrieved on July 31, 2024 from https://americafirstpolicy.com/issues/research-report-reversing-the-woke-takeover-of-higher-education-strategies-to-dismantle-campus-dei

Probyn, E. (1996). *Outside belongings*. Routledge.

Putnam, R. (1993). What makes democracy work? *National Civic Review, 47*(1), 101–107.

Putnam, R. (2000). *Bowling alone: The collapse and revival of American community*. Simon & Schuster.

Putnam, R., Leonardi, R., & Nonetti, R. (1993). *Making democracy work: Civic traditions in modern Italy*. Princeton University Press

Saugestab, S. (2004). The indigenous peoples of Southern Africa: An overview. In R. Hitchcock & D. Vinding (Eds.), *Indigenous peoples' rights in Southern Africa* (pp. 22–43). Eks/Skolens Trykkeri.

Smith, D. (2024). *Diversity's promise in higher education—Making it work* (4th ed.). John Hopkins University Press.

Somerville, P. (2011). Democracy and participation. *Policy & Politics, 39*(3), 417–437. https://doi.org/10.1332/147084411X581817

Taylor, J. (2024, September 11). Labor's plan to ban children from social media might actually create more harm, charity says. *The Guardian*. Retrieved on 14 September 2024 from https://www.theguardian.com/media/article/2024/sep/12/australia-plan-to-ban-children-from-social-media-might-actually-create-more-harm-charity-says

Tosun, J., & Julia Leininger, J. (2017). Governing the interlinkages between the Sustainable Development Goals: Approaches to attain policy integration. *Global Challenges, 1*(9). https://doi.org/10.1002/gch2.201700036

UNESCO. (2024). *Fossil hominid sites of South Africa*. Retrieved on 3 September 2024 from https://whc.unesco.org/en/list/915/

United Nations. (2013). *A new global partnership: Eradicate poverty and transform economies through sustainable development* (Report of the High-Level Panel of Eminent Persons on the Post-2015 Development Agenda).

References

United Nations. (2015). *Resolution adopted by the General Assembly on 25 September 2015.* Retrieved on 15 August 2024 from Microsoft Word—1516301E.docx (un.org). https://documents.un.org/doc/undoc/gen/n15/291/89/pdf/n1529189.pdf

Valodia. I. (2023, September 15) *South Africa can't crack the inequality curse. Why, and what can be done?* University of Witwatersrand News. Retrieved on 8 September 2024 from https://www.wits.ac.za/news/latest-news/opinion/2023/2023-09/south-africa-cant-crack-the-inequality-curse-why-and-what-can-be-done.html

Vincent, A. (2001). Liberalism and citizenship. In M. Evans (Ed.), *The Edinburgh companion to contemporary liberalism* (pp. 51–62). Edinburgh University Press.

Wahlquist, C. (2017, July 5). Map of massacres of Indigenous people reveals untold history of Australia, painted in blood. *The Guardian.* Retrieved on 1 September 2024 from https://www.theguardian.com/australia-news/2017/jul/05/map-of-massacres-of-indigenous-people-reveal-untold-history-of-australia-painted-in-blood

Van Krieken, R. (1999). The barbarism of civilization: Cultural genocide and the 'stolen generations.' *British Journal of Sociology, 50*(2), 297–315.

Wang, Y. P., & Kennedy, K. (2023). Regime-supporting or regime-challenging? Chinese secondary students' intentions for future political participation. *Citizenship Teaching and Learning, 18*(1), 7–22.

Wilson, S. (1997). *Bringing them home: National inquiry into the separation of Aboriginal and Torres Strait Islander children from their families.* Human Rights and Equal Opportunity Commission.

Windschuttle, K. (2009). *The fabrication of Aboriginal history Vol 3: The stolen generations 1881–2008.* Macleay Press.

Ying, J. (2021). Political participation as self-cultivation: Towards a participatory theory of Confucian democracy. *European Journal of Political Theory, 20*(2), 290–311. https://doi.org/10.1177/1474885117751763

Yuval-Davis, N. (2006). Belonging and the politics of belonging. *Patterns of Prejudice, 40*(3), 197–214.

Open Access This chapter is licensed under the terms of the Creative Commons Attribution-NonCommercial-NoDerivatives 4.0 International License (http://creativecommons.org/licenses/by-nc-nd/4.0/), which permits any noncommercial use, sharing, distribution and reproduction in any medium or format, as long as you give appropriate credit to the original author(s) and the source, provide a link to the Creative Commons license and indicate if you modified the licensed material. You do not have permission under this license to share adapted material derived from this book or parts of it.

The images or other third party material in this book are included in the book's Creative Commons license, unless indicated otherwise in a credit line to the material. If material is not included in the book's Creative Commons license and your intended use is not permitted by statutory regulation or exceeds the permitted use, you will need to obtain permission directly from the copyright holder.

Chapter 5
Life Education: Educating Citizens for Disruptive Futures

Abstract Traditional forms of school-based civic education are no longer enough to prepare for disruption in future. Citizenship education must now become education that continues throughout life. This chapter argues that the concept of lifelong learning is not appropriate for this task. Life education, as discussed earlier in this book, is proposed as the new way to think about citizenship education throughout life. There will be challenges throughout the lifespan and these are discussed as well as the need for action in both preparing for disruptions and confronting them directly. The concept of 'action with moral intention' is introduced as the kind of action needed in future since it will guide the values behind confrontation to support the needs of the most vulnerable in society.

Keywords Citizenship education · Life education · Moral intetnion · Values

5.1 Introduction

Citizenship education is traditionally thought of as something done in schools and therefore for children and young people. Yet these are not traditional times. Russian aggression in Ukraine has been ongoing for over two years, Israel has been waging war against Palestinians and Lebanese in response to Hamas's attack on Israel over a year ago. Iran has been brought into this conflict on account of its support for Hezbollah, a well-known opponent of Israel. Coupled with these geopolitical conflagrations is the constant degradation caused by climate change, the unpredictable impacts of AI, especially in relation to the labour market, the continuing rise of right wing and divisive politics influencing what has been described as "democratic backsliding." On account of these contexts, a new way of thinking about citizenship education is required in order to confront the issues facing the twenty-first century.

Traditionally, citizenship education has come in various forms such as civic education, moral education, political education, religious education, ideological education and more. In different jurisdictions, these may be separate subjects, integrated studies, extra-curricular activities or a combination of these. Despite there being a common

© The Author(s) 2025
K. J. Kennedy, *Disruptions and Civic Education*,
SpringerBriefs in Citizenship Education for the 21st Century,
https://doi.org/10.1007/978-981-96-5875-6_5

commitment across countries to the idea of citizenship education, these various forms suggest that no one is quite sure how best to organize learning for citizenship. If this is the case for traditional forms of citizenship education, it is even more so for the kind of education needed to support citizens in confronting disruptions. Citizenship education for disruption is only on the agenda in sporadic ways—education for climate change, energy education, anti-poverty education, education for gender equity. What is needed is a more holistic approach that recognizes the scale of future disruptions and the necessity for equipping citizens to confront them.

The first step in considering the kind of education needed for current and future citizens is to understand that this is not just a matter for children and young people. Education is needed for all citizens and it needs to be continuing education. In the past, much attention has been given to the idea of "lifelong learning" to the point where its importance is now taken for granted. Yet there is little depth in the idea when it comes to confronting disruptions. Education cannot be a stop-start process and it is not optional: it must start and never stop. The issues to be discussed in this chapter are related to the shape that education can take and how it needs to become part of a world readying itself for disruption. The following areas will be discussed:

- From 'lifelong learning' to life education: Citizenship education as a moral enterprise
- Life education as pragmatic curriculum action
- Multiple citizenship education challenges across the lifespan
- Restrictions on action—limitations and boundaries
- Education for 'action with moral intention'
- Learning-Lessons from the front line.

5.2 From 'Lifelong Learning' to 'Life Education: Considering Citizenship Education as a Moral Enterprise

5.2.1 Lifelong Learning

Lifelong learning emerged out of a series of papers and policies within what was originally the European Community (EC) and subsequently the European Union (EU). The key issue identified as early as the 1970s was in a statement issued by the EC (Pépin, 2007):

> A genuine awareness has emerged of the importance of the links between education and the economy and of the development of systems of further training and permanent or continuous education. (p. 124)

By the middle of the first decade of the twenty-first century "lifelong learning 'from cradle to grave' was…the guiding principle of the integrated Education and Training 2010 work programme" (p. 129). This link between education and the economy is now well known within both policy and practitioner circles. Sometimes it is seen to reflect an instrumental view of education as opposed to a more progressive or humanistic view. This tension is an important one to understand in seeking an approach to the future education of citizens.

In one sense, seeking to educate citizens to confront future disruptions is itself an instrumental role for education so there is nothing intrinsically wrong with instrumental purposes. Yet 'lifelong learning' is more than instrumental: it is embedded in multiple theoretical spaces that construct it in different ways. Frąckowiak (2017) argued that UNESCO's view (as outlined above) represents "the humanist view on lifelong learning, (focusing) …on changes in society and labour market, highlighting the individual, but in the broader context of community" (p. 4). A definition by Longworth and Davies (1996) reflected this humanistic perspective:

> Lifelong learning is the development of human potential through a continuously supportive process which stimulates and empowers individuals to acquire all the knowledge, values, skills, and understanding they will require throughout their lifetimes and to apply them with confidence, creativity and enjoyment in all roles, circumstances, and environments. (p. 22)

As opposed to this humanistic perspective is a neoliberal view that has found expression in multiple global institutions such as OECD, the European Commission and the World Bank. Fejes (2009) argued that under neoliberalism an individual is regarded as:

> an autonomous, self-choosing and self-regulating self who should take responsibility for his/her own life… (and) the 'state' is constructed as the 'enabling state' which should make it possible for the citizens to make their own choices. (p. 383)

Over time and globally, UNESCO's humanism was replaced by OECD's neoliberalism fuelled by globalization and the emergence of what has been referred to as the 'knowledge economy'. Neoliberalism occasioned two dominant responses to this economic landscape. The first was to replace responsibility for responding to changes caused by globalization on individuals (thus the importance of lifelong learning which was seen as an individual responsibility) and secondly, removal of any responsibility for support from the state. Fejes (2009) referred to this as "neoliberal governmentality" (p. 385). This is not what is needed to confront disruptions. Such confrontations require collective responses and the full-hearted support of government. There is little doubt that learning is central to confronting disruptions. The issue is to consider a replacement for neoliberalism's lifelong learning' as a driver for citizenship education.

5.2.2 Life Education

It is difficult to identify Western sources that help to identify the origins and characteristics of life education. Nevertheless, Tan et al. (2021) identified Chinese scholars who argued its origins were in the United States in 1960s as a response to multiple social problems (p. 118). Taiwanese scholars, on the other hand, trace its origins to Taiwan (p. 119). Whatever its origins, there is abundant evidence of the adoption of life education as a major curriculum theme in China, Hong Kong and Taiwan (Lee et al., 2021; Zhao & Lee, 2024; Zhao et al., 2024). The main structural characteristic of life education as a curriculum option is that it has been focused on schools, although Tan et al. (2021) pointed out that there have been extensions into universities. Within schools, life education is located within the general area of moral and values education. Yet it is not possible to be more specific than this since in different locations life education takes on distinctive characteristics. It is this diversity, however, that makes life education a potentially powerful component for citizenship education.

The diversity of approaches to and understanding of life education has been well documented (Zhao & Lee, 2024). Yet little attention has been paid to how different views might be integrated into a more holistic understanding. Table 5.1 outlines a possible integrated approach to considering life education.

The descriptions of life education shown in Table 5.1 are a selection from diverse literatures. Yet the categorization of these descriptions under broad "types" is more stable reflecting different ways of thinking about life education. A further analysis of these types will provide a foundation for thinking further about life education and its capacity to support the education of future citizens.

5.2.2.1 Life Education as Transcendental

Sun and Lee (2021) pointed out that in the first phase of the development of life education in Taiwan there were three focus areas:

- Ultimate concern and ultimate practice, which involve the construction of life philosophy and the exploration of issues related to thanatology as well\ as religions.
- Ethical thinking and reflection, which deals with issues related to basic and applied ethics, and
- Exploration of integrity as integration of the physical, mental, and spiritual aspects of the whole person (p. 43).

The reference to "thanatology" reflects Taiwan's initial concerns with death education and grief as an aspect of life education. This was not an exclusive concern for developers of Taiwan's earliest form of life education. Japanese educators had similar concerns concerning death education (Ikezawa, 2019; Katayama, 2002) and Mainland Chinese scholars are also aware of its importance (Niu & Du, 2024). Such a focus indicates that life education was a considerable diversion from the academic curriculum conceived as very broad in its scope, dealing with issues beyond the everyday and concerned with a holistic view of life rather than one defined by the narrow aims of traditional schooling. Over time and in different locations, this focus has not always been maintained but it is an important one to keep in mind.

Table 5.1 An integrated approach to life education

Type	Description	Location	Reference
Transcendental	Concerned with the meaning of life as well as everyday life	Taiwan, Japan	Sun and Lee (2021) Iwata (2017)
Protective	Linked to social issues like public security education, safety education, national defence education, education for sustainable development	Mainland China	Tan et al. (2021)
Pragmatic	Health education, moral and ethical education, environmental and citizenship education, religious and spiritual education	Hong Kong	Lee et al. (2023)

5.2.2.2 Life Education as Protection

Table 5.1 shows three examples of life education as protection—protection of the individual, protection of society and protection of the state. Niu and Du (2024) provided a good example of life education as individual level protection by linking it to the mental health of students:

> Schools should, through daily teaching and school activities, gradually strengthen elementary school children's awareness of life, their knowledge of health, their appreciation of the preciousness of life, and the development of their mental health and sense of well-being. Children should be well prepared to adapt to an unknown social life in the future. (p. 90)

This is not the kind of knowledge students will encounter in math, science or social studies. It is a different kind of knowledge: it is knowledge about life, with a focus in particular on the value of life.

Yet individuals live in a social context and life is more than the challenges they confront personally. Climate change, poverty, discrimination, for example, are issues that face a whole society. One the one hand, these can be seen as academic issues that have involved a great deal of research. On the other, they can also be seen as political issues that have created considerable tensions within societies. Yet over and above these two ways of looking at these issues, they are also issues about life: the quality of life, the fairness of life and potential threats to life. Education about these topic can be viewed as socially oriented life education and there are many examples.

Climate change curriculum (Woodard & Schutz, 2024), education for sustainable development (Sass et al., 2024), anti-racist education (Kincaid, 2024) and anti-poverty education (Gorski & Landsman, 2013) have all been the subject of attempts to engage students in both understanding the issues and where necessary taking appropriate action. The action component is important since that directly involves students' lives. Becoming engaged means students are learning that they can protect themselves while also acting to support others. They are also learning about the issue and understanding its significance. Knowledge and action are the key components of life education as protecting both individuals and society.

5.2.2.3 Life Education as Pragmatic Curriculum Action

The most recent review of the school curriculum in Hong Kong under the general heading of "Values Education and Life Planning Education" recommended to (Task Force on Review of School Curriculum, 2020):

> Accord higher priority to values education in schools, including strengthening life education, and moral, civic, and national education (MCNE); and start life planning education early at the upper primary and junior secondary levels. (p. 16)

Here life education is embedded with a range of other strategies to support the development of young students. This approach is described as an "holistic and integrated approach for promoting different facets…of VE" (p. 17). In a subsequent graphic of this approach, seventeen separate values are identified ranging including "sex education, consumer education, civic education, anti-drug education and national education." Life education is added to this diverse list as one among many value systems that can contribute to both personal and social development. From a values perspective, this is the most pragmatic approach relying on multiple ways to educate for the future rather than a single dimensional approach.

An important issue to consider is whether among the seventeen different values endorsed by the Hong Kong curriculum reform, does life education have a distinctive role to play? At one point, the reform document highlights an objective for life education:

> to cultivate in students a care for life, and positive values and qualities for meeting unanticipated crises as well as helping them to develop a strong sense of civic-mindedness and social responsibility. (p. 17)

In terms of the previous discussion, this is a combination of life education as individual protection and life education as social protection. This reinforces the pragmatic approach in which life education can serve multiple purposes. What is more in the 'seventeen value approach' mentioned earlier there are other values with a similar objectives such as "moral and ethical education, media education, basic law education, human rights education" (p. 17). Thus, life education within a pragmatic framework does not carry the entire values load—this load is distributed across multiple learning areas.

5.2.3 Life Education—From Concept to Application

Niu and Du (2024)'s statement that "life education is education throughout one's life" (p. 87) challenges the school-based nature of life education as outlined throughout this section. What is more, it offers an alternative to lifelong learning and its accompanying neoliberal connotations. Life education is not only about life—it is for life. It should start in schools, but in future it should not stop there. Table 5.2 shows how the basic conceptual understanding of life education could be translated into a broad curriculum framework capable of facilitating citizenship development.

Table 5.2 Life education framework for citizenship development

A transcendental aspect	Looking beyond the self for answers about life and living	This will vary from context to context. It may include religion (or religions) or spirituality or ideology. How do people look outside themselves for support and development?
A protection aspect	Protecting the world starting with the individual and including society and the environment	Three possible dimensions: *Personal*: How do I protect myself? *Social*: How do I protect society? *Environmental*: How do I protect the environment?
A pragmatic aspect	Acknowledeging there are multiple sources of knowledge, skills sets and values that can interact to support individual and society	Valuing more than ethnocentric knowledge and cultures to acknowledge multiple knowledges, values and skills that can support future development

This framework represents the starting point for a curriculum discussion about a citizenship education that could prepare young people for a disruptive future. An important point to make is that the framework is not about the school curriculum only: it is about a citizenship education for life. The framework is not itself a curriculum yet it can provide the basis for discussing what is appropriate content including knowledge skills and values. Before considering more detailed curriculum possibilities based on this framework, it is important to acknowledge that any form of curriculum development takes place within specific contexts. These contexts will be explored in the following sections before coming back to consider more explicit curriculum formulations for life education across the lifespan.

5.3 Multiple Citizenships and Education Challenges Across the Lifespan

Table 5.2 is deliberately generic to cater for both interdisciplinarity and multiple implementation contexts. Citizenship is also generic and can be applied to people's lives wherever they may happen to be. Yet discourses on citizenship are not generic. They will differ depending on where individuals are located. In countries such as the United States, the United Kingdom, Australia, France, South Africa and many more, those discourses will be around citizenship education for democracy. Citizens will be encouraged to participate and to contribute to social and political development. In other countries such as Pakistan, Saudi Arabia, the United Arab Emirates, Indonesia, Malaysia and many more, citizenship and religion will be intertwined. Good citizens in these contexts will be committed first to their religion. There are yet other countries not concerned with either democracy or religion but are nevertheless anxious for citizens to support the political regime and its values often without providing citizens with any choice. These three broad types of contexts for citizenship produce very different discourses about responsibilities, behaviours and values. As shown in Table 5.3, a spectrum of contexts for citizenship can be identified based on the three broad outlines above. Requirements for being a citizen differ in the contexts outlined in Table 5.3. The challenge is whether the framework outlined in Table 5.2 can be applied across these multiple contexts. An important reason for raising this issue is that disruptions will not consider contexts but will have the same effect irrespective of them. How might citizenship education designed to confront disruptions work in these different contexts?

The contexts shown in column 1 of Table 5.3 are best understood as political in nature and often the discourse concerning them highlights the differences between them. For example, democratic contexts highlight freedom for individuals and engagement in the political system. On the other hand, authoritarian regimes are more likely to require obedience from citizens and commitment to regime values. There is often an evangelical zeal in democracies seeking to 'convert' other political systems to the democratic cause. It is unlikely these tensions can be easily resolved or will disappear. What is more, disruptions will not distinguish between regimes: all political systems are facing the same challenges and these challenges demand a response.

Responses to disruption must be in the form of action—governments need to take action; non-government organizations of multiple types need to take action; and individuals need to take action. Can the political regimes outlined in Table 5.3 facilitate such action? It might be argued that action is more likely to take place in democratic regimes than in authoritarian because freedom has a more central role to place in democracies. While such an argument may have had some face validity in previous times, it cannot be allowed to characterize what needs to happen currently. Thus, within the framework outlined in Table 5.2 I want to include a focus on action as a key characteristic of citizenship education in future. I shall argue this case below,

Table 5.3 Contexts for citizenship

Contexts	Description	Examples
Liberal democracy	Commitment to values such as equality, human rights, universal suffrage, freedom	United Kingdom, France, Australia, South Africa
Illiberal democracy	Universal suffrage but much less commitment to other democratic values	Hungary, Türkiye, Bulgaria, Croatia, Serbia
Democracy & religion	Liberal democratic values place as outlined above are in place but religion plays a very significant role in the lives of citizens	Pakistan, Malaysia, Indonesia
Religion	Religion is the dominant element in citizens' lives	Iran, Afghanistan
Authoritarian	Commitments are to the state and its preservation	China, Russia, North Korea

not so much from a theoretical perspective but from the practical perspective: without action, disruptions will win.

5.3.1 Action and Life Education

Waghid (2005) referred to "action as an educational virtue" (p. 323). He dismissed liberal and communitarian notions of citizenship while also critiquing both Habermas' and Young's views of discursive and radical forms of democratic citizenship. For Waghid, it is Nussbaum's and Greene's ideas of 'compassionate' and 'imaginative' action that best provide for the foundation of a citizenship education focused on reconciliation. His views are best understood in the context of South Africa's racialized history and the development of a democratic state designed to overcome past injustice and create a new inclusive and just society. The focus of his argument, therefore, is on individuals and their interactions. Understanding the 'other' is of utmost importance and connecting with the experience of 'others' is the beginning of what Waghid (2005) calls "civic reconciliation" (p. 325). Yet for our present purposes we need to go further than the individual, although Waghid's analyses will be helpful in considering the nature of actions in a broader citizenship context.

For Waghid (2005), when a student initiates a discussion point in class this can be regarded as 'action'. It is based on a personal decision to engage, to have a voice and to connect with others. Confronting disruptions, however, requires a broader framework for action that can take multiple issues into consideration. Jann (2024), concerned with "climate change and sustainability education and practice" (p. 1), drew on Aristotle's concept of *phronesis* to propose two key concepts that should guide action in these areas:

> the *ability* to judge—some moral, ethical and/or normative sense by which one choice is valued over another, and the knowledge, skills, and means to make that choice; and *should do* - to not just act but have both the moral need to act and to act according to both values and competency. (p. 3)

These two concepts embody the essence of phronesis that "taps into the changing world of contingents, and is concerned with practical reasoning about particulars, the end of which is action.... yield(ing) decisions…each of which embodies a correct prescription or right reason for a given set of circumstances" (Darnell et al., 2019, p. 112). It is this link between action and moral intention that is important to understand. Action is not ad hoc in any way and it is not merely 'clever' (Darnell et. al., 2019, p. 113). Action and virtue must be linked, and while this does not exclude 'clever' solutions such solutions must also be virtuous solutions (Darnell et al., 2019, p. 113). Such an approach is consistent with John Rawls' (1999 [1971]) view that civil disobedience should be "non-violent and conscientious" (p. 320) and Martin Luther King's view that no progress had been made in the civil rights movement "without determined legal and nonviolent pressure" (The Texas Politics Project, 2024). Yet several issues related specifically to *phronesis* need to be understood.

There are two main points to consider. First, going back to an ancient Greek philosopher in order to provide a framework for confronting twenty-first-century disruptions may seem counter-intuitive. Focusing civic thinking and action towards moral intention, however, requires ways of thinking that differ from the largely secular contexts that has constructed citizenship education in Western contexts. Apart from the emergence in recent times of character education, Western forms of citizenship education have been dominated by secular values handed down from the European enlightenment and eventually transformed by the emergence of postmodernity. This was demonstrated in the earlier discussion of Waghid (2005) and his championing of post-structuralist solutions to major social problems. Such solutions focus entirely on the needs of individuals and their desires with little attention paid to broader social contexts and pressing needs within those contexts. Moral intention disappeared from Western discourse in general and citizenship education in particular. Thus, the resort to an ancient Greek philosopher!

Second, however, the retreat of Western discourses and theories from considering moral intention in civic decision making does not reflect a universal situation. In East Asian contexts, Confucianism has kept morality at the centre of citizenship discourse. Lee (2004) pointed out:

> Rather than talking about politics, citizenship education in the East talks about morality. 'Civics' always goes with 'morals' in the East, thus civic and moral education is a term more common that civics education or citizenship education in Asian countries. (p. 32)

Lee and Kennedy (2024) showed how extensive this moral turn was motivated by Islam in some Asian countries, Buddhism in others and a broad commitment to spirituality as a motivating force across multiple societies. As Kennedy and Lee (2021) pointed out, the European Enlightenment was just that—a European phenomenon that did not extend beyond its borders. There has been no equivalent "Asian Enlightenment" to break the links with religion as happened in Europe. Thus, what may seem like a moral turn in modern Asian thinking is in fact a reflection of traditional Asian values. Confucianism, for example, continues to exert effect even in China where its values are now seen as consistent with those of the ruling Chinese Communist Party. *Phronesis*, therefore, should come as no surprise to those societies for whom moral intention has always been a dominant feature in life generally and citizenship in particular. Yet the linking of moral intention with action many not always be welcome as shown the following section.

5.4 Restrictions on Actions—Limits and Boundaries

A briefing note by a government agency highlighted the ambivalence that even democratic governments have about direct action (Downs, 2024):

5.4 Restrictions on Actions—Limits and Boundaries

> An individual's right to freedom of expression and assembly are protected by Articles 10 and 11 of the European Convention on Human Rights. Together they safeguard the right to peaceful protest. However, these rights are not absolute, and the state can implement laws which restrict the right to protest to maintain public order or protect the rights and freedoms of others.

This could easily be a statement issued by one of Europe's illiberal democracies or even by an authoritarian state like Russia. Yet it actually came out of a review by the UK's House of Commons. Using this notion of "rights are not absolute", Kier Stammer's new Labor government quickly moved against what he called "far-right thuggery" (Whitehead, 2024) as groups of protestors attacked asylum seekers and others across multiple English towns. In Australia, the Prime Minister attempted to stop protests by groups of Palestine supporters protesting against humans rights violations in Gaza. The courts allowed protests to proceed under specific conditions, but the Hamas flag was not allowed as part of the protest and images of the recently slain Hezbollah leader, Hasan Nasrallah, were not allowed to be displayed. The point I want to make is that even within mature democratic societies, where freedom is often seen as a core value, there are limits. Such limits are often contested, as was the case when the Australian Prime Minister wished to stop the pro-Palestinian protests all together, but limits were eventually imposed although not the extent the Prime Minister wished. Yet there is another issue about the examples described in this paragraph.

In both the English and Australian examples, there were significant moral issues involved. England's Prime Minister did not regard unprovoked attacks on significantly disadvantaged community groups as rights consistent with the Human Rights Act. The right to peaceful protest is guaranteed under the Act, but the English example showed that hate-inspired protest does not meet this criteria. In the Australian context, Prime Minister Albanese "was incredibly worried about social cohesion" and argued Australia was not a place "for the waving of terrorist symbols" arguing that "we need to promote social cohesion in our multicultural nation" (Hyland, 2024). He took this position despite a very strong human rights tradition in Australia and a guarantee under the law for freedom to protest peacefully. Like his UK counterpart, the Australian Prime Minister signalled that from his perspective moral intention overrode broad legal guarantees.

Such an approach will always be contested, but part of its importance in the context of this chapter is that the events described above took place in mature democracies. There are limits in these contexts just as there are in other regimes, although the limits in non-democratic regimes will obviously be greater. But who can forget the anti-COVID-19 protests in China in November 2022 followed by the lifting of restrictions in December? Amnesty International (2023) identified over 20,000 anti-war activists in Russia, despite state crackdown on them. In Iran, women continue to protest against laws requiring them to wear the hijab though the actions of the "morality police" charged with the responsibility for policing Islam law (Rajvanshi, 2023). Acting in these contexts will always be difficult, but moral intention is a strong motivating force and it is such intention that should be brought to bear in confronting future disruptions.

Yet we need to be realistic. There are examples throughout history where moral intention was the motivating force for action but the results were not immediately forthcoming: Ghandi in India, apartheid activists in South Africa, freedom fighters in the southern states of the United States and anti-Vietnam War protestors in many Western countries. Each of these cases faced considerable opposition from governments and law enforcement agencies. Participants often faced great odds. The use of attack dogs against civil rights protestors in Birmingham, Alabama, in 1963 (Willis, 2023) and the non-judicial killings that characterized the apartheid regime in South Africa are extraordinary examples of moral intention being thwarted by naked power and immorality. These powerful and negative influences will not disappear from human interaction, but they do not abrogate the importance of acting with moral intention.

5.5 Educating for 'Action with Moral Intention'

Facilitating action for moral intention in contexts that might not always be receptive requires careful attention to building both skills and understanding across time and place. A basic curriculum framework was outlined in Table 5.2 and this can be expanded by considering additional experiences that would prepare not just young people but adults as well. The focus is on location from 'self' through to the 'global'. More work is needed to integrate the original framework (Table 5.2) with what is outlined below (Table 5.4) and together they indicate how civic learning can be developed to prepare citizens for disruption.

The Learning Areas in Table 5.4 are expanded below.

Table 5.4 Civic learning for the future: acting with moral intention

Learning area	Description
1. Personal, Social and Environmental	1.1 Individual wellbeing 1.2 Social engagement and responsibilities 1.3 Environmental Action
2. Institutions	2.1 Institutions and values 2.2 Experiencing institutions 2.3 Institutions and actions
3. Learning in the community as well as about the community	3.1 The community as a learning resource 3.2 Learning in the community and classroom 3.3 Action in the community
4. Learning globally	4.1 Learning about others 4.2 Learning about peace 4.3 Intercultural learning

5.5 Educating for 'Action with Moral Intention' 111

1. *Personal, social and environmental learning*

Civic learning is multifaceted and it is important to explore the full range of associated knowledge, skills and values. These are more likely to be reflected in integrated learning than single subject learning but the form civic learning will take need not be prescriptive.

1.1 Individual Wellbeing

Often civic knowledge is abstract and far removed from the lives of individuals. As part of life education, individuals must know themselves, what affects them and how to balance conflicting pressures in daily living. These processes should go on throughout life so that a highly functioning individual can contribute in the best way possible.

1.2 Social engagement and responsibilities

Individuals live in society and have a responsibility to contribute to it. There are many avenues by which this can be done starting with the family and ending with society as a whole. Service learning is one way of doing this throughout life and so too is engagement in the political system. These kinds of servant leadership are important for society as a whole.

1.3 Environmental action

The environment now creates eco-anxiety for individuals and society and the need for action at multiple levels is essential. Many young people see the need for action as a social rather than a political imperative. This social imperative is an important way to protect society. Individuals can take environmental action in simple ways and should be encouraged to do so throughout life in order to relieve eco-anxiety and restore planetary balance.

2. *Learning about and in institutions*

2.1 Institutions and values

Institutions reflect a society's values. Legislatures, courts, executives, police forces, armed services, civil service, religious organizations and schools are core institutions in most societies, although names, functions and histories differ. Throughout life individuals need to understand how these institutions work, their purposes and how they can assist in the development of society.

2.2 Experiencing institutions

Institutions are not abstractions but organizations that rely on individuals to fulfil their purpose. At a young age, individuals can visit them, ask questions about them and learn about them. At later stages, they can become formal members and contribute in substantial ways. Experiencing institutions will provide understanding of their role and function in society.

2.3 *Institutions and actions*

Institutions are action organizations that involve multiple activities that can contribute to the development of society. These activities need to be for the good of society: laws to respond to climate change, school curriculum that help students understand injustice in society and ways to confront it, regulations to protect individuals from unscrupulous practices and much more. It is the task of individuals to oversee these actions and assist institutions to achieve their moral purposes.

3. *Learning in the community as well as about the community*

3.1 **The community as a learning resource**

The community contains all that is necessary for life and living. Communities consist of businesses, professionals, industries, schools, churches, non-government organizations, sporting venues, movie theatres, transport and more. These resources all have educational value in one way or another and can contribute to both formal and informal learning.

3.2 **Learning in the community as well as classrooms**

For young people, classrooms have become centres for learning despite that learning often takes place way beyond them. Classrooms have been convenient over time. But the full potential of the community needs to be developed especially since learning is throughout life. Adults can meet together anywhere in the community to engage in learning opportunities, and young people do not need to be confined to classrooms when resources are available in the community. Learning can be encouraged as an activity of daily living rather than an activity confined to classrooms.

3.3 **Action in the community**

Communities should not be passive entities or simply responsive to external events. They must be places of action whether it is about the environment, school values, support for the poor or other areas that can support the positive development for community members. Positive communities are likely to provide the foundation for positively oriented citizens.

4. *Learning globally*

4.1. **Learning about others**

We may live within borders and the narrow confines of a single nation state, but modern life transcends these borders. This is true in terms of communication, travel, employment opportunities and more. Global engagement means it is important to focus learning on places, people and possibilities for living beyond the nation state as well as within it.

4.2. **Learning about peace**

Peace is most often talked about as the opposite of war, and certainly peace is the preferable way to live in this world. Yet living in a state of peace is also an individual state of being. This idea is advanced by different religions and spiritual philosophies. Young people and adults need to learn about these dimensions of peace and what they mean both for the planet and for individuals.

4.3. *Intercultural learning*

Learning to respect others is at the heart of intercultural learning. Global engagement inevitably brings people into contact with a broad range of people in different cultures and with different values. The same can occur within countries that have diverse populations. Learning about other cultures, learning to respect them and learning the value of difference are key priorities for twenty-first-century citizens.

Curriculum development takes time, deliberation and engagement with ideas and concepts. What is presented above and earlier represents the beginning of a conversation about a new approach to curriculum for citizenship education. Hopefully over time the ideas will be developed to suit unique contexts and the needs of citizens confronted with disruptions. This kind of curriculum development represents our hope for the future.

5.6 Learning-Lessons from the Front Line

The extension of citizenship as part of life education requires a deep understanding of the role and purpose of learning, for both young people and adults. The final section of this book is an ideal place to consider what is required in terms of learning that can support efforts in confronting disruptions. What follows applies particularly to adult learning, but the principles apply equally to the kind of learning schools should be encouraging.

Extended forms of citizenship education are not about the accumulation of more and more civic knowledge (what Freire would call "the banking model of learning"). Rather, it is about a heightened understanding of the need for change and new ideas. Each scholar approaches this priority from a slightly different angle. Two perspectives have been chosen to demonstrate this point: those of Paolo Freire and Antonio Gramsci. While coming from different contexts and with differing perspectives, their overall message is consistent: the status quo is inadequate and there is a fundamental need to expand thinking about what is needed for the future.

5.6.1 *Lessons from Freire*

Lawton (2022) described Freire's critical pedagogy as a means "to awaken and expand the consciousness of poor and oppressed peoples around the world" through "consciousness raising processes", referred to as "conscientization" (from the Portuguese, "conscientização" (p. 50) defined as:

the process of moving from naive or passively received understandings of self, others, and the world to more critical and active understandings, of moving from partialized or focalized views of reality to a more total and contextual view of reality. (p. 50)

Out of this understanding came *Pedagogy of the Oppressed* (Freire, 2010), the work for which he is best known among educators. Yet Armitage (2013) pointed out that 'conscientization' is about more than the motivation for learning:

…rather its concerns are focused upon individuals becoming critical, enlightened citizens capable of critically engaging with and transforming the world. (p. 3)

It is in this broader sense that conscientization is relevant here as the driving motivation of twenty-first-century adult education and the driving force of life education. This is quite different from the origins of adult education in nineteenth-century England. At that time, the mass education of the population was seen as an instrumental process related to the development of literacy skills and the capacity to read the Bible (thus saving the souls of working people!) (Hudson, 1851). The twenty-first century requires citizens who can transform society in order to confront multiple disruptions. Conscientization as defined above is the process that can facilitate that process as a learning principle related to life education but particularly for adult learning.

5.6.2 Lessons from Gramsci

Freire acknowledged his debt to Gramsci (Mayo, 1999) but it went beyond their shared belief in Marxism. Both reformers had a strong belief in the efficacy of education to bring about change. Mayo (1995) argued that "Antonio Gramsci saw in the education and cultural formation of adults the key towards the creation of counter-hegemonic action" (p. 145). Mayo (1999) identified "transformative theor(ies) of education" (p. 17) as key link between them. What this term implies is that education needed to be transformed if societies were to achieve change. The status quo would not be sufficient—a view shared equally by Freire and Gramsci.

For Gramsci, this basically meant the education of workers so they could understand what needed to be done to secure a better future. In addition, he also felt they needed to understand the kind of culture that fed current inequalities in society. This was about the preparation of workers who would have responsibilities once the hegemonic capitalist system was overthrown.

This is not the sense in which transformative education is used in this chapter. Rather, it borrows from Gramsci (and Freire) the radical nature of transformative education as education that challenges the status quo and seeks new understandings. The purpose is not so much to throw of the yoke of hegemonic capitalism, as with Marxism. Rather, the purpose is to use life education as the means of equipping citizens to confront current and predicted disruptions with new knowledge, new skills and new values. Freire and Gramsci would argue that political systems may inhibit this process, but this is an old formulation. Political systems will not outlast disruptions. In the current global context, therefore, transformative education will have a role in educating those systems as well.

The world has changed a great deal since Freire and Gramsci advanced their thinking about the importance of transformative education. Yet the need for such education has not changed and indeed has become more urgent. Continuing with the status quo is not an option, old knowledge and ideas are not options, and old values are not options. Moving forward, transformative approaches are needed to confront new times and new challenges. This is a significant challenge for citizenship education in future.

References

Amnesty International. (2023). *Russia: 20000 activists subject to heavy reprisals as Russia continues to crack down on anti-war movement at home*. Retrieved on 10 October 2024 from https://www.amnesty.org/en/latest/news/2023/07/russia-20000-activists-subject-to-heavy-reprisals-as-russia-continues-to-crack-down-on-anti-war-movement-at-home/

Darnell, C., Gulliford, L., Kristjánsson, K., & Panos, P. (2019). Phronesis and the knowledge–action gap in moral psychology and moral education: A new synthesis? *Human Development, 63*(2), 101–129.

Armitage, A. (2013). Conscientization, dialogue and collaborative problem based learning. *Journal of Problem Based Learning in Higher Education, 1*(1), 1–18.

Downs, W. (2024). *Research briefing—Policy powers: Protests*. Retrieved on 8 October 2024 from https://commonslibrary.parliament.uk/research-briefings/sn05013/

Fejes, A. (2009). Fabricating the lifelong learner in an age of neoliberalism. In M. Simons, M. Olsson, & M. Peters (Eds.), *Re-reading education policies: A handbook study the policy agenda of the 21st century* (pp. 375–388). Sense Publishers.

Frąckowiak, A. (2017). A review of lifelong learning as natural and cultural phenomenon. *International Journal of Psycho-Educational Sciences, 6*(2), 1–11. Retrieved on 22 September 2024 from https://files.eric.ed.gov/fulltext/EJ1254643.pdf

Freire, P. (2010). *Pedagogy of the oppressed. 30th Anniversary edition* (M. B. Ramon, Transl.). Continuum.

Gorski, P., & Landsman, J. (Eds). (2013). *The poverty and education reader: A call for equity in many voices*. Routledge.

Hudson, J. (1851). *The history of adult education*. Longman, Brown, Green & Longman.

Hyland, J. (2024, October 2). Pro-Palestinian events will go ahead in Sydney if prohibited by NSW Supreme Court, organizers say. *ABC News*. Retrieved on 10 October 2024 from https://www.abc.net.au/news/2024-10-02/prime-minister-anthony-albanese-sydney-palestinian-protest/104421182

Ikezawa, M. (2019). The development of thanatology in Japan and its position in East Asia, with a focus on thanatology's relationship to religion. *Numen, 66*(2–3), 114–138. https://doi.org/10.1163/15685276-12341535

Iwata, F. (2017. Life education and religious education in national, prefectural and other public schools in Japan. In M de Souza & Halafoff (Eds.) *Re-enchanting education and spiritual wellbeing. Fostering belonging and meaning-making for global citizens* (pp. 86–96). Routledge.

Jann, J. (2024). Phronesis in climate change and sustainability education and practice: Importance of the immeasurable goodness of a professional. *Sustainable Development*. [*First Online*] https://doi.org/10.1002/sd.3089.

Katayama, A. (2002). Death education curriculums for elementary schools in Japan. *Illness, Crisis & Loss, 10*(2), 138–153. https://doi.org/10.1177/105413730201000204

Kennedy, K., & Lee, J. C. K. (2021). Religion, modernities and education, contexts for Asia's religions. In K. Kennedy & J. C. K. Lee (Eds.), *Religious education in Asia; Spiritual diversity in in globalized times* (pp. 1–11). Routledge.

Kincaid, M. (2024). *Freedom teaching: Overcoming racism in education to create classrooms where all students succeed*. Wiley.

Lawton, P. (2022). Paolo Freire's "conscientization." *RoSE, 13*(1), 49–65.

Lee, J. C. K., & Kennedy, K. (2024). Searching for peace in a Troubled word. Life and values education in Asia: Introducing the Handbook. In J. C. K. Lee & K. Kennedy (Eds.), *The Routledge international handbook of life and values education in Asia* (pp. 15–19). Routledge.

Lee, J. C. K., Yip, S. Y. W., & Ho, R. M. K. (2021). Introduction: Life and moral education in the Greater China region. In J. C. K. Lee, S. Y. W. Yip, & R. H. M. Kong (Eds.), *Life and moral education in Greater China* (pp. 1–38). Routledge.

Lee, J. C. K., Zhang, E., & Liu, R. (2023). Life and values education: Beyond the self. In K. Kennedy, M. Pavlova & Lee, J. C. K. (Eds.), *Soft skills and hard values—Meeting education's 21st century challenges* (pp. 112–132). Routledge.

Lee, W. O. (2004). Emerging concepts of citizenship in the Asian context. In W.O. Lee, D. Grossman, K. Kennedy & G. Fairbrother (Eds.), *Citizenship education in Asia and the Pacific—Concepts and issue* (pp. 25–36). Comparative Education Research Centre, The University of Hong Kong/Kluwer Academic Publishers.

Longworth, N., & Davies, W. (1996). *Lifelong learning: New vision, new implications, new roles for people, organizations, nations and communities in the 21st century*. Kogan Page.

Mayo, P. (1995). Antonio Gramsci and adult education. In C. Danis & M. Hrimech (Eds.), *Adult education: The past, the present, and the future* (pp. 148–154). Proceedings of the 14th Annual Conference of the Canadian Association for the Study of Adult Education Montreal, Quebec, Canada, June 1–3. Retrieved on 20 October 2024 from ED394010.pdf.

Mayo. P. (1999). *Freire, Gramsci and adult education—Possibilities for transformative action*. Zed Books.

Niu, J. J., & Du, J. (2024). A study on the implementation issues and strategies of life education in primary schools. *Curriculum and Teaching, 7*(5), 87–92. https://doi.org/10.23977/curtm.2024.070512

Pépin, L. (2007). The history of EU cooperation in the field of education and training: How lifelong learning became a strategic objective. *European Journal of Education, 42*(1), 121–132.

Rajvanshi, A. (2023, July 17). What the return of the 'morality police' means for Iran's women. *Time*, Retrieved on 10 October 2024 from https://time.com/6295238/iran-morality-police-return/

Rawls, J. (1999 [1971]). *A theory of justice*. Belknap Press.

Sass, W., Maeyer, S., Boeve-de Pauw, J., & Van Petegem, P. (2024). Effectiveness of education for sustainability: The importance of an action-oriented approach. *Environmental Education Research, 30*(4), 479–498.

Sun, J. H. C., & Lee, J. C. K. (2021). The philosophical basis of life education. In J. C. K. Lee, S. Y. W. Yip, & R. H. M. Kong (Eds.), *Life and moral education in Greater China* (pp. 41–61). Routledge.

Tan, C. B., Zhao, Z., & Lee, J. C. K. (2021). Understanding life education in Mainland China: View through the lens of moral-civic education. In J. C. K. Lee, S. Y. W. Yip, & R. H. M. Kong (Eds.), *Life and moral education in Greater China* (pp. 118–130). Routledge.

Task Force on Review of School Curriculum. (2020). *Optimise the curriculum for the future foster whole-person development and diverse talents final report*. Education Bureau. https://www.edb.gov.hk/attachment/en/curriculum-development/renewal/taskforce_cur/TF_CurriculumReview_FinalReport_e.pdf

The Texas Politics Project. (2024). *Martin Luther King, Jr. and organized civil disobedience*. Retrieved on 28 October 2024 from https://texaspolitics.utexas.edu/archive/html/ig/features/0607_01/slide3.html

References

Waghid, Y. (2005). Action as an educational virtue: Toward a different understanding of democratic citizenship education. *Education Theory, 55*(3), 323–342.

Whitehead, J. (2024, August 3). *Another day of chaos across England*. BBC News. Retrieved on 8 October 2024 from https://www.bbc.com/news/live/c0jqjxe8d1yt

Willis, M. (2023). The police dog as weapon of racial terror. *JSTOR Daily*. Retrieved on 11 October 2024 from https://daily.jstor.org/the-police-dog-as-weapon-of-racial-terror/

Woodard, R., & Schutz, K. (2024). *Teaching climate change to children: Literacy pedagogy that cultivates sustainable futures*. Teachers College Press

Zhao, Z., & Lee, J. C. K. (2024). Contexts and orientations of life education in Asia. In J. C. K Lee & K. Kennedy (Eds.), *The Routledge international handbook of life and values education in Asia* (pp. 20–29). Routledge.

Zhao, Z., Lee, J. C. K., & Tan, C. B. (2024). Life and values education in China. In J. C. K. Lee & K. Kennedy (Eds.), *The Routledge international handbook of life and values education in Asia* (pp. 106–114). Routledge.

Open Access This chapter is licensed under the terms of the Creative Commons Attribution-NonCommercial-NoDerivatives 4.0 International License (http://creativecommons.org/licenses/by-nc-nd/4.0/), which permits any noncommercial use, sharing, distribution and reproduction in any medium or format, as long as you give appropriate credit to the original author(s) and the source, provide a link to the Creative Commons license and indicate if you modified the licensed material. You do not have permission under this license to share adapted material derived from this book or parts of it.

The images or other third party material in this book are included in the book's Creative Commons license, unless indicated otherwise in a credit line to the material. If material is not included in the book's Creative Commons license and your intended use is not permitted by statutory regulation or exceeds the permitted use, you will need to obtain permission directly from the copyright holder.

The manufacturer's authorised representative in the EU is Springer Nature Customer Service Centre GmbH, Europaplatz 3, 69115 Heidelberg, Germany. If you have any concerns regarding our products, please contact ProductSafety@springernature.com

Printed and bound by CPI Group (UK) Ltd, Croydon, CR0 4YY

26/03/2026

02078975-0004